LETTERS LONGED

MERAKI ARTISTS

To The Artist In Every Person.

Compiled By,

Anuksha Arge and Himanshu Kamble

Contents

Contents

Contents

Contents

Contents

Preface

Handwritten letters are the most personal and cherished ways of expressing love. Just how the buds wait for the sun to bloom, a writer's words are like letters a reader awaits. Waiting, means what or whom you're waiting for matters; sometimes so much that it consumes a lifetime. Waiting is rare, but so are people that do it out of love and longing of their beloved. Words are help and so, We have stitched together the spine of this book that you're holding and filled each page with letters, poems and stories written by helping hands from different places on this planet that will hold you dearly.

Acknowledgements

Meraki Community

We, Meraki Community, are from the Nagpur city. We actively stage open mic events, in which we lovingly showcase various talented artists art forms which include, spoken word poetry, storytelling, singing, standup comedy and many more. Taking a step ahead in showcasing our immensely talented poets and writers, we thought of publishing their writings in a book.We succesfully published an anthology called 'Bound To Last' last year. Bearing the same thought in mind, we came forward with this one too. We are

ACKNOWLEDGEMENTS

deeply thankful to all the amazing writers and poets for supporting us. You can connect with us on Instagram - @meraki_community_

People Behind Meraki

Sanskar Samarth

Hi! Sanskar Samarth here I'm 19 and pursuing my engineering in E&TC branch. I'm an amateur writer, and I find peace by writing my heart out, and I love perform, it's my dream to perform in front of huge crowd. You can follow me on Instagram - sanskar.samarth this is my I'D. Thank you!

Anuksha Arge

I'm 20 and pursuing Bachelors in Physiotherapy from VSPM College. Above all that I love, like doing theatre, writing and performing poetry, reading. dancing. photography, painting, traveling, I love living life to the fullest , most! I believe that our lives are incomplete without love and purpose. Meraki is close to my heart and so, it is my purpose to help it grow and inspire talents and to provide them the value they deserve. To read more of my poetry @_theanuquoted_ _@annukshaaa_

Himanshu Kamble

I'm 22 and pursuing my Engineering in (ETC) from GHRCE College. I started writing to express my feelings and emotions through words. Meraki is really close to my heart its 3 years now while I'm working with meraki, In upcoming years you will see meraki at completly different level, for that me and my team is really working hard. It's one of my dream to make this community prominent in all over India.

Sakshi Mahajan

I'm Sakshi Mahajan nd I'm 22 year old from Nagpur. I write poetries it's not my hobby bt I'm in love with this Poetry connects me with people glad that people Relate it with their life. I write what I feel and Poetry is something that gives me peace, happiness, nd love from people which motivates me to write more. This is the best way to tell people about your life nd your thoughts regarding love, life, and a lot of things. you can't learn how to write poetry. but yes you can learn a lot from it. If u ever wanna listen or read my words u can check out my writeups here:- @sakshimahajan

1. Shikwa Rab Se

Kya tu vakayi hain wahaan,
Dua karta tujhse sara jahaan.

Kyo hain tu sota, jab tera banda hain rota.
Tujh par toh nahin hain koi bediyaan,
Durr kyo nahin karta tu ye andheriyaan.
Rab se upar na usne kisi ko maana,
Phir kyo na jeene de use ye zamaana.
Giri, royi, uthi, giri.
Chalte rahein ye kisse.
Kyo hain dard aur na khushiyaan, uske hisse.

Kyo aas lagwayi tune, agar nahin thi isme teri marzi.
Kaisa hain tu, kaisi hain ye teri khudgarzi.

Kehte hain tu banata hain jodiyaan, tu milwata insaan ko.
Gamo ke badal bhale aadmi ko, kya deta haiwan ko.
Kaafi der kar chuka hain,
Haq ki uski khushi kab dega insaan ko.

Ta-umra umeed leke wo chalta raha,
Chaaye ghane baadal, raaste me kaatein, magar wo badhta
raha.
Sach toh ye hain ki usne sirf gam hain paya.
Tu toh hain sartaj, tera faisla mujhe samajh na aaya.
- Bhawna Arora

Bhawna Arora

I am a businesswoman living with all the zeal and strength to achieve the best and always aspiring to grow in life in all dimensions. Proud homemaker and manager to my family serving them all the love and support.
Insta - @sonal_speaks

2. Cached

Often when I look at you I wonder
What's lost in your smile ?
appears as a burning starfire
yet you shy away
it's fluttery warmth gives me faith
but shrinks you anyway
How it stirs a paradox to our brains
to me seeks an inward joy
To you it masks.
Little do you know
How I long to stray in it
Only if you'd let me
And not stow it away.
- Mehak Pant

3. Deluging Amour

How beautifully does the rain remind me of you
The tune of the pouring water reminds me of the soft hugs that
caress the soul
The cold breeze makes me miss the warmth of your breath.
With every sip of the warm tea
Do I remember the essence in the intensity of your love
The eyes filled with unexpressed love
The thoughts deep withing the sea of hearts enclosed with
emotions
The weaving dreams of a comforting future.
Oh how I remember the dormant love inside of me , the love
that's not expressed
The love that yearns but can't be said
Rains are the times my heart craves to feel the warm desires of a
sweet completion
Admires the beauty in your eyes
but mostly prays for a Neverending lingerness of your soul in
mine.
- Mehak Pant

Mehak Pant

Hii, I'm mehak

A budding poetess

someone who is only writing if she's by a window.It all started
from journal writing to consolidating it into remembering
moments I would cherish reading even on my last days.
Writing for me has a life to itself.From the first word till the
last,you live those moments,feel those emotions all over again
everytime you read it experiencing that is divine.
There's more to this hopeless romantic side of me.
Instagram : @meheck._

4. MS Dhoni – The Crown Jewel Of Indian Cricket

On 23rd December 2004, the cricketing world witnessed the beginning of an incredible era in Indian cricket. The 23 year old wicket keeper batsman from Ranchi, Mahendra Singh Dhoni made his debut for India in an ODI against Bangladesh in Dhaka. But his beginning in international cricket could hardly be referred to as a fairy-tale. In fact, it was the stuff of nightmares. He began his international career with a duck, getting run out in his first match. In his next 3 matches, he recorded a string of low scores which made everyone doubt the calibre of this new-comer in Indian cricket. There were even rumours that he will lose his place in the Indian team in the upcoming tour where Pakistan was scheduled to play in India. The night before the second ODI in Kochi, Indian captain Sourav Ganguly called MS Dhoni and told him that he was going to play the game. This gave Dhoni a lot of confidence. In this match, India were batting first and MS Dhoni was promoted to the number 3 position. This move from Captain Ganguly marked the entry of a champion. MS Dhoni had finally arrived! He scored a whirlwind 148 runs from 123 balls and India went on to win this match comfortably. His wicket keeping too impressed everyone and soon enough he

became a permanent fixture in the Indian team.

In the coming years, the entire cricketing world started to fear this long-haired boy from Ranchi whose batting prowess and match finishing abilities started gaining momentum. All opponent teams against whom India played were witness to the dominance of MS Dhoni. He started winning games from impossible situations. The world had seen the birth of a new kind of a wicket-keeper batsman. His inputs to the bowlers, especially spinners, often proved to be very valuable and he developed a reputation of having an excellent cricketing mind.

It was the year 2007, where India had just finished a horrific ODI World Cup campaign in the West Indies, where India registered defeats from teams like Bangladesh and Sri Lanka, thus marking their exit from the World Cup. The cricket frenzy nation of India was in a state of shock! Everyone was looking for the revival of Indian cricket after this disastrous campaign. The inaugural edition of the T20 World Cup was to be played in South Africa in the month of September 2007. Everyone was very excited as it was the first time such an experiment was being conducted in cricket.

It was expected that a senior Indian talisman will be picked as the captain for this tournament. However, the selectors thought out of the box and announced the name of MS Dhoni! The rest as they say is history. India went on to win this World Cup and a group of young boys led by an innovative captain had conquered the world. The message to the world was loud and clear. 'MS Dhoni: Captain Cool' began a glorious journey to take Indian cricket to newer heights.

As a leader, Dhoni was very calm and composed. He was a great reader of the game and one of the finest tacticians that cricket has ever produced. Sometimes he was unorthodox in his approach, but he always had a very clear vision of his targets and how he needed to achieve them. By the end of 2008, Dhoni became the Indian captain across all the three format, the first cricketer to achieve this feat. This meant that he would be minutely scrutinized for his each and every move. Every decision that he took on the field was keenly observed by millions of cricket fans. This was a big challenge, but as they say, 'When the going gets tough, the tough get going'. Dhoni took to captainship beautifully. In his early years as the captain, he had the support of great veterans like Sachin Tendulkar, Rahul Dravid and VVS Laxman. With such prominent seniors, the team also had a blend of very talented young cricketers like Virat Kohli. Under Dhoni, the Indian team started winning a lot of series in home as well as in away conditions. In the year 2009, the Indian test team rose to the number one position in ICC rankings. This was a big slap to all those critics who felt that Dhoni was a good captain only in the limited overs formats. From 2009 to early 2011, the Indian team performed brilliantly in all the three formats everywhere in the world. The year 2011 was going to be extra special, and it would go on to mark one of the most special sporting moments in the 21ˢᵗ century in India.

The world cup campaign started for India with a victory over Bangladesh and the Indian juggernaut rolled on seamlessly. All the opponents barring South Africa (where India lost) and England (where the game ended in a tie) were defeated by the Indian team. In form Sachin Tendulkar and Zaheer Khan, a string of brilliant all-round performances by Yuvraj Singh and excellent leadership by MS Dhoni were some of the important factors due to which India was able to dominate the World Cup. India defeated Australia in the quarter finals and arch rivals Pakistan in the semi-final. The date for the biggest clash in cricket was set. On 2 April 2011, India was set to face off against Sri Lanka in the World Cup final.

This was undoubtedly the biggest game of all the cricketers present in that match. 2 best teams of the tournament were set to take on each other in a battle of cricketing supremacy. After MS Dhoni lost the toss in this crucial encounter, Sri Lanka elected to bat first. Riding on the brilliant performance of Mahela Jayawardena, Sri Lanka posted a first innings total of 274. Reeling at a score of 114 for 3, the in-form Yuvraj Singh was expected to come in to bat. But Captain Dhoni had something else in his mind. Despite being out of form he decided to promote himself to the number 5 position. He played a match winning knock of 91 runs and hit the famous six off Nuwan Kulasekara to lift the World Cup. It was the first time that a team playing in home conditions had won the world cup and it was a moment of triumph for all to cherish.*

In the coming years MS Dhoni achieved many remarkable feats in his illustrious career and led the Indian team from the front. The most notable achievement was when the Indian team lifted the Champions trophy in England in 2013. This made him the only captain till date to lift all the ICC trophies, a record he still holds. He led the Indian team for almost a decade with grace and a style that earned him accolades from the entire cricketing fraternity. He will serve as an inspiration to all the players and captains in the years to come.

To conclude, it is correct to say that the legacy of MS Dhoni goes far beyond his victories. Now that he has decided to hang his boots, the world of cricket is sorely missing one of its finest champions. It is very hard to measure the tremendous impact that Dhoni has had on Indian Cricket. He has set the bar very high for his successors to conquer. His fantastic achievements coupled with a very down to earth behaviour have made him one of the greatest icons of Indian sports. If every upcoming cricketer is able to follow in the footsteps of Mahendra Singh Dhoni, the game will be much the richer one.

- Nilay Narsikar

Nilay Narsikar

An Avid Reader, a Hodophile and a Cricket Buff, these are the things I am deeply passionate about. I also have a keen interest in the political affairs of India and the World. To share my ideas, experiences and feelings, I sometimes turn to writing which showcases a glimpse of my persona. So dear readers, I welcome you to a snippet from my world and wish everyone a happy reading

For more, feel free to reach me on IG: nilaynarsikar_7

5. Toh Fir Tumse Mohabbat Hi Sahi!

Kate ke us par se Kate ke is par ke aam se lagne wale tum kab khas bante chale gaye iska anuman bhi mai kuch ghadiyo bad hi lga payi hu . wo kahate hai na ki apko kisi ki choti se choti bat bhi pasand aa sakti hai to kisi ka bade se bada sach bhi apko swikara nhi jayega ! jivan me naya kand hone wala hai , theher jao ldki , tham jao keh kr tum se najre milayi . us ek lamhe me tum mehej ' tum ' nhi the ! mere chehere ki wo udasinta mano khilkhila kr hasne ki firak me thi . sukun mehej shabd nhi reh gya tha mano sukun se mai rubaru mulakat kr rhi thi . ankho ka chamkna , ayne me khudko savarna , or hotho ki laali ye kuch kuch aisa hi tha jaise kisi bacche ko uska manpasand khilone ko dekh hui hlki si chatpatahat. Aayne me tircha tircha dekh ankhe uchkakar tumse bate krna kya sadharan bhasha me bhi utna hi khubsurat lgta ?

labzo se chipta sach ankho se baya hona to tay tha , mai lakh mna kr lu khudko pr ye to sach tha na ke us pure vakt meri ankhe kisi pr thi to vo ' tum ' the !

tumse kitna kuch kehena tha or shayd sunna bhi . na bhooto na bhavishya pr ha tum mera vartman the jise mai hr ek sukshm kan me jiya hai . laga nhi tha ki yeh kahungi pr ha farak to padta hai , tumhara hona ankho ka ek khubsurat sa dhoka keh lo ya fir dilasa keh lo pr isme mere jivan ke un taman satyo se kayi adhik rahat hai.

Aksar mai kahaniyo ko adhura nhi chodti pr khudko sach se pare nai soch bhi kaha pati hu. jab jab tumse milungi tab tab is kahani ke kuch panne fir bhar diye jayenge tumhari yaado se . khair , shayad iska koi ant nhi hai ; or shayad iska adhura hona hi ise asal mayne me pura banata hai . or agar ise mohabbat kehete hai to fir tumse mohabbat hi sahi!

- Kajal Maroti Kapgate

Kajal Maroti Kapgate

(The girl who talks in poetry)
I'm a student of UG besides I'm a passionate writer. I always lost in my thoughts without which I'm incomplete. My writings encourage me to share some glorious moment and my indefinite thinkings to the world. at the end I got closer through my poetry.

6. Talash Hai Uski!

Jisko muskurane ki wajah na chahiye ho
Jo bewajh apna bachpana dikhati ho
Jo is fake si duniya me bhi khushi se jeeti ho
Jo Star bucks ki coffee nahi mere saath baith kar chai piye!
Haa talash hai uski !

Jisko baarish me bheegna pasand ho, usse dekhne se jyada,
Jo tumhe janti ho khud se jyada.
Haa talash hai uski !

Jo apni chize chunne me bhale hi ulajti ho,
Lekin tumhari har uljan ko shuljhane me tumhara saath deti
ho!
Jo is bhid bhari duniye me tumhara haath padak kar kahe "is
haath ko kas ke pakadlo abhi bohot lamba rasta katna hai
hume"
Haa talash hai uski !

Jiske saath baate karke mai apne shamo me aur rang bhar saku
Jiske saath baith kar koi shikwe mehsoos na ho
Haa talash hai uski!!
Jiska pyaar adhoora rahe lekin Radha - Krishna jaisa pura hone

chahiye
Haa bas talash hai uski!!
- Sanskar Samarth

Sanskar Samarth

Hi ! Sanskar Samarth here I'm 19 and pursuing my engineering in E&TC branch. I'm an amateur writer, and I find peace by writing my heart out, and I love perform, it's my dream to perform in front of huge crowd. You can follow me on Instagram - sanskar.samarth this is my I'D. Thank you!

7. I hope you are fine there

I grown up in your arms
We played together in your farms;
I remember the time you breathed for the last
Never knew people would fly too fast.
You kept feeding me by your hand
Scolded when I accidentally ate sand
You took me to the bed on time
And you slept forever as if I did any crime?
You loved me like your own child
I cried remembering the last day you smiled;
With all the lessons you added to my memories
I hope,you are now resting in peace !
Chocolates,gifts and dresses you brought
The only epitome of love I got
Your blessings kept making me stronger
But the day you left I cried a little harder.
Till the another ride in that toy train
Grandpa,I will miss you until we meet again.
- Shreya Narayan Chaple

Shreya Narayan Chaple

Living beyond the limits is what I prefer. Writing with emotions is what I found when you don't know where life takes you to. I Shreya Narayan Chaple, a 19 years old girl with billions of emotions and thoughts inside which prefers to express feelings by writing and not by speaking it out. Where people find love in person, I found love in writing and this is what makes me complete. 11 years of writing and still looking forward for more. Instagram - @she.leaves.mystery.__

8. Bebas Betiya

Reh gai vo Gumsum Apne Khwab na vo Saja Pai, Aye Khuda Tu Hi Bata us Nanhi Si bacchi ne kin Karmon ki Saja Pai? Roti bilkhti, Hasti khelti vo apni maa Ki god Mein, Kyu usene Maut Ki Saja Pai? jakar Poochho Koi uss baap se Jisne apni Nanhi Pari Gawai, Aye Khuda Tu Hi Bata us Nanhi Si bacchi ne kin Karmo ki Saja Pai? Jisne Nanhe Pairon se Chalna na Sikha, na hi vo ye Duniya dekh Pai, Kyo in darindo ko Tune Khuda dedi itni chaturai?, kii chhin kar Kisi Pari ki Muskan Hawas Ki Jisne Pyas mitai, Aye Khuda Tu Hi Bata us Nanhi Si bacchi ne kin Karmon ki Saja Pai? kya biti Hogi use maa per Jo apni kaleje ke tukde ko Na bacha Pai, Khwab sajaye Honge use Jab Nanhi Si Pari Thi unke Ghar aai, kyu Insaniyat mein iss darindagi ka Daag Laga Hai?, Ab To Krishna Tumhen aana hoga, Yahan hajaron Draupadiyo ka Jivan dav per Laga Hai, ho sake to Punh Mahabharat rachao, O Kanha Punh laaj Yahan bikane se pahle Tum a jao., Beti Bachao Beti padhao ki Yahan Kasam Thi Sab Ne Khai, Kahan Gaye Sare Jab vo Nanhi Si Jaan per Aach thi aai?, Bhari Hogi Kai siskiya usene aur Shayad awaaz bhi hongi Lagai, Kyon Krishna us Samay vahan Tumne chir Nahin Badhai, Aye Khuda Tu Hi Bata us Nanhi Si bacchi ne kin Karmon ki Saja Pai? Aye darindo Tumne sirf Pyaas na apni bujhai hai, Aaj Tumne insan ke roop mein haiwaniyat

Dikhai hai, iss haiwaniyat ko apni Jeet na samajhna, khabardar upar wale ke dar per jakar Unse mafi ki ummid Na Karna, Ki le li Chuppi Sare shasan prashasan ne, Bhul Gaye Shayad Maa Aur betiyan Khuda Ne Di Hai unke bhi daman mein!, kapdon per Dekho Zara Kisne ungali uthai hai, Kii chaar sal ki Masoom ne bhi to apni masumiyat Gawai hai, Na Jane Kab Tak Meri betiyan Draupadi ban lut ti Rahegi, Krishna Tum a jao Ek Bar ki chir To Nahin badh Rahi Insan mein Insaniyat Kyon Dino Din h Ghat Rahi, Shabd bahut hai Par na Jaane Kyon main na Keh Pai, Jawab De Insan kahan se Tujh Mein haiwaniyat aai?, ab Bahut Hui betiyon per Nahin chalegi AaTtai, Aye Khuda Tu Hi Bata us Nanhi Si Pari ne kin Karmon ki Saja Pai?

- Poonam Sharma

Poonam Mishra

Hey I'm Poonam Sharma, a Poet by mood, may be these sounds somthing weird or different but my situations and mood motivated me to write something about my life or about that am surrounded with. In a day to day life as a girl who grows up in indian family or society we faces many problems, we hear many things like, u can't do that ,you don't have to wear like this ,u can't live your life as u want or they(so called society)set up limits for our life but dear girls we are flying birds,add wings to your dream and fly high to touch the sky,and make your desire your *destiny, don't give your key of happiness to someone's hand.Instagram - _imperfect_thoughts_writing_*

9. Advancement in Science and Technology It's "Impact on Human Evolution"

We all know Human species are the most intelligent species on EARTH . Being intelligent species isn't enough to survive for a long period but we should also be able to evolve according to the environmental changes. Do you think we "HUMANS" are evolving as required to maintain our long dominant reign on MOTHER EARTH ? In this Article I'm just sharing my views how I feel about advancement of science and technology effecting our Evolution. Firstly, What is Evolution meant in General? Evolution is nothing but " Biological changes occurring in body to adapt and survive accordingly to our environmental changes.

" Now in Scientific terms,

Evolution is change in the heritable characteristics of biological populations over successive generations. Different characteristics tend to exist within any given population as a result of mutation, genetic recombination and other sources of genetic variation. Any species takes centuries to evolve, by the process of Natural selection, genetic mutation or any other means leading the species to get adapt to Environmental conditions allowing it to survive. The species which can't adapt or stoped evolving eventually become extinct. Every living species depending on their geological location, availability of food and resources available varies from it's own species in other location.

For example look at Elephants. "African elephants" are larger in size and also have larger ears compared to "Asian Elephants". Elephants have huge body and thier ears are biologically engineered like fins, where the blood flows to ears and gets cooled and circulates back in to body to maintain optimum temperature. We know in African regions the temperatures are high compared to Asian regions this is the one of the reasons for bigger ears of African elephants than that of Asian. Likely are the bears and polar bears differ. So the species of lions and other species including Humans.

"Advancement of science and technology" is a good thing but DO YOU AGREE IT IS HELPING US IN PROCESS OF EVOLUTION?

I guess it's just cutting us out of natural evolution. Let me give an example how it's stoping us. The "rising temperatures" globally are the effects of environmental change if we aren't developed this far in science we may haven't know the "Air-conditioning". The human species now are using AC in hotter regions and Room Heaters in cold regions resulting in relying more on artificial comfort zone i.e., We are creating man made environment for comforting ourselves.

Now if we aren't developed this far our body's may adapted to changing temperature and environment around us. Yeah in old days we have fire to warm up our bodies but warming our body by natural process would help us to sustain until we got mutated to adapt to environment naturally.

However we are now creating our own environmental comfort zones and stoping ourselves to mutate or evolve like the other species.

These are my views on where we are in the process of evolution. I'm not against the development of Technology but we are more relying on them which may result in a trouble in Human species evolution process.

- *Known Stranger*

10. Life without living

Having a nice career, a good status and being in respectable position in the society we name them as Responsible and Successful people in life.
Have you ever thought, why only we "Humans" need to build a career, live a fake life and worry about the society around us.

Every creature on earth around us is born to explore the world. May be this career, society and status is just our creation and is just a myth.

One day, I wish all of us move out of this circle and explore our life in the nature, there by know the real purpose of life and create the world with real and new life.
- Known Stranger

11. Unexpressed Soul

When expressions of soul left unspoken,
My actions of love inked into words,
Hoping to reach your heart.
- Known Stranger

Anjan Kumar

May be I'm known by my name and face yet I'm stranger by my thoughts and views.

*I'm Known Stranger. Instagram - @stranger_writings_*

12. Love, As I Know It

Sometimes you don't choose love but love chooses you.
When you truly love someone you don't love them for their looks,
you love them for their vibe, their heart.
They jump in your life silently like the ordinary people but by
time they make you realise that they are not ordinary one they
are special.
Just a call or text from them is enough to keep you happy
throughout the day. Even an hour feels like a minute when you
are with them.
They accept who you are and not what they want you to be, with
all your imperfections and flaws they will still choose to be with
you.
Sometimes you can't explain what you see in a person it's just the
way that they take you to a place that no one else can.
- Himanshu Kamble

Himanshu Kamble

I'm 22 and pursuing my Engineering in (ETC) from GHRCE College. I started writing to express my feelings and emotions through words. Meraki is really close to my heart its been 3 years now while I'm working with meraki, In upcoming years you will see meraki at completely different level, for that me and my team is really working hard. It's one of my dream to make this community prominent in all over India.

13. Safarnama

Ye adhuri Mohabbat jaruri thi janaab
Warna yakin maniye hum alfaazo mein ye Dard kaha se laate
Apni har aah pe waah waahi kaise paate Jo mili nhi
Uss Mohabbat Ko har pal Bhala kaise jee paate
Isliye ye adhuri Mohabbat jaruri thi janaab
Unka woh bas muskurana, unki woh khamoshi woh intezaar
Hamari har nazm Ko hawa de Raha tha
Mil jaate woh toh behak jaate hum
Ye ishq hame darasal hamari Manzil de Raha tha Khali ehsaaso
ki ye tijori
Jahaa ishq ki Daulat hai behisaab
Yakeen maniye ye adhuri Mohabbat jaruri thi janaab
Ek ek Lamhe ka bikhar ke yu sadiiya ho Jana
Unki awaaz ka yu Kayal ho Jana
Kayi mauke ijaar ke phir bhi kuch Naa keh pana
Unke har Andaaz ka rago mein yu ghulte Jana
Unke liye likhe khato ka unn tak Naa pohoch paana
Beshumaar ishq ka bas ek tarfa Re jana
Dhoondhte Rehna uss unkahe sawal ka jawab
Isliye ye adhuri Mohabbat jaruri thi janaab
Ab roj tumhe jeete hai
Ab roj tumpe marte hai

Tum miloge ya nhi iss baat se bhi ab kaha darte hai
Meri har nazm ka Tum aaiya ban baitho ho
Ki shakal meri hai par wajood Tum ban baitho ho
Tumse dur jaane ki khwaish ki thi kabhi
Ki kuch yu dua kabool hui
Tumse dur tumhe saath le aaye hum
Ishq toh ishq naam bhi tumhara odhe baitha hai khubsurat
nakaab
Bas samjh lo ki isliye hi ye adhuri Mohabbat jaruri thi janaab
Ye adhuri Mohabbat jaruri thi janaab
- Tejal

Tejal

Writing my heart and building homes
Instagram - @Rjtejal

14. Strangers

Two strangers, Old by their age.
Sat on an old bench, with their legs stretched.
They both had a glance, with two little smiles.
Legs getting cold, by the cold tiles.
The corridor was empty, just a breeze of cold.
It is about to snow, as they were told.
Not a single word uttered, yet shared a thousand words.
Who said we need to speak up ?
Voices of each other's that they never heard.
They both share a bidding smile, as they got released from pain.
The other one said, Until we meet again.
- Kshitij Deshmukh

Kshitij Deshmukh

Exploring my self as a writer. Not a full-time poet, but tried my luck in it.

Instagram - @biblio_writeups

15. Asaan Zindagi

Agar Zindagi asaan hoti to khuda jannat ka wada karta ,
Tum ya mai uske dar pe apne khaoishe ka boj na tikate,
Apne gharo ko kafilo se naa batte,
Jarre-jarre me ranjishe nahi bandhte,
Asman tak tukdo me nahi ginte,
Matti ke hr tinke me insano ka nam nahi likhwate,
Rango se khalishe nahi sikhate,
Wo rehmat ki chadar ek sa phailata sab ke sir pe,
Na kam na jiyada, na mehenga na sasta,
Sab ek sa, sab ek se, sab ek dua ke nam,
Nam hazar q na ho, pr yaad karne pe ek hi dehleez pe therthi
ankhe.
Aur fir bhi kehte hum, khuda bada khudgarz hai.
Pr sach to aisa hai ki hum hi insaan khudgarz hai,
isilye to wo khud aur garziyan alag dekh na saka aur ussi
ko khudgarz therane chala.

- Oshin Shahare

16. Ikraar

Mausam-ae-bhul teri inayat se jiyada teri muskurahat pe Fida
ho chale,
Tum pe ye ungliya rukhne se pehle labon pe aa rukhi,
Wo bahon me ye jo lipte jism
Pal bhar ke liye bhul jaye sari khidmat,
Uth sa gaya tha tere shehar se bharosa,
Pr tumhari mulaqaton ne fir pighla diya iss pathar dil ko,
Ab to tumhari parchai se bhi ho chala h pyaar,
Ghadi ke kate bhi lagte ab arson se,
Jin palkon se hua tha pyaar pehli nazar me,
Ab unse ye nazre fir ek dafa milane ki hai jaldi,
Arzu ye bhi hai ki tumhare laute waqt captain - tumhari train
thodi aur late ho jaye,
Ha, tumhi se hui hai mohabbat.
Haan, tumpe ake rukhi hai ye nazrein.
Pr Ishq se bhi jiyada humari haseen mulaqaton se hui h ye
binkash ikraar ki shuruaat ye jarrur!
- Oshin Shahare

17. Muntazir

Tumse mohabbat hone se pehle teri mulaqaton se ho chali thi,
Tumhari gheri ankhe samundar ke lehro jaise sukoon sa paigam
rakhti hai,
Wo shafeeq ankhon-hi-ankhon me ahihsta batla gaye ki unhe*
meri jism se pehele mere balo se ho chala hai ishq,
Un labon ka kya kehna jo ruh se pehle Dil ko chu jaye,
Akhir na-umeed se umeed rakhna inhi ne to sikhlaya,
Kaise meri hasi uske yado ke canvas me apni jagah bana gayi,
Tum nazro me khel gaye sahab , hum to Aaj bhi tumhare itar ke
nashe me Kaif-ae-iztarab ho rakhe hai,
Tumne batao me guzare un palo ko, aur ye dil ne tumhe khud
me utara,
Beshaq tumhare pass distraction bahot se hoge,
Pr mujh sa haseen to jaroor na hoga,
Itne dino ke baad bhi tumhare sukoon me lipat ke shame
guzarna ,yahi dili tamanaa muntazir hue baitha nadan dil.
Kuch iss tarah tumhare saye ke ehsaas ko pyaar ki siyahi se naksh
kiya mere yaado ke ek panne me.
- Oshin Shahare

18. Proposal

Ab har waqt uski tasveer ko takte ghante nikal jate,
Usse Milne ki betabi ab man ke juthe kisse bunne laga hai,
Pichli mulaqaat me use keh bhi na payi ki uski chuhan sabse
anokhii hai ,
Kaise uske baho me hifazat hai,
Akhir kaise kehti, thodi pata tha wo mulaqaat lambi judai ke
sath free thi,
ab to uske khayal bhi aa jate binsoche hi,
Reh-reh ke Usme mera aaj dikhne laga hai,
Kaise kahu ki uski mulaqate sabse ache kisso se the, uske jane ke
baad bhi uski khushboo mere kambhal me uski tarz rakhti thi,
Agli baar se pehle mujhe Usse kuch kehna hai ki, Suno - Suno,
ha mana pichli baar hath tumne thama tha, par iss bar mujhe
thamna hai tumhara sath, kaho iss weekend free ho to mile.

- Oshin Shahare

19. Andheri Raat

Waqt ka kuch aise khayal rakhta Mai,

din bhar ke shor me auro sa ghulta,

manzil Andheri raat tak ka safar kuch aise bitatata-

Ungliyon me ginne jitne humari mulaqaton thi, siyahi banake

kuch kisse utare hai kagaz ke tukde pe,

Haar raat thodi udaan deta unhe,

Kabhi haal, to kbhi tumhari chal se karta wakif me unko,

Timtimati Raton me bhi , tumhari chuhan ki alamat se jagi

rakhta in ankhon ko,

Soch ke kisi din mere dairy se udd ke tumhare hath me aye ye

khayal to,

Ho sake to, ho sake to- tum bhi apna haal batla ke , haule se

apni khushboo aur waqt sang Lana,

Uu tatolta mai andheri Raton se din ke ujale tak, waqt ka kuch

aisa khayal rakhta Mai apne sang.

- Oshin Shahare

20. Khudgarz Mai

Ye zalim duniya usse badnam thehrati rahi,
Ab mai dar-dar kaise samjhau iss duniya ko,
Usne nahi balki maine hi mussal usse iss jhuthe pyaar ke nam se
sare zamane me badnam kiya,
Yahi ab jabta hu dar dar jake, abki baar uss darbar me bhi
batlana hai,
Jiske sirane matha tikane ke baat uski akhri khawaish thi,
Yahi ab jabta hu dar dar jake,
abki baar uss darbar me bhi batlana hai.
- Oshin Shahare

21. Sirf Tum

Yuhi tum manate rehna ,
Meri har nasamzi harkato pe,
Kya hua kabhi chai jara si ubal ke niche gir jaye ya koi chez tut
jaye na jaan ke,
Tum please muskurake kandhe Yuhi uchka dena,
Yuhi tum pyaar dikhlate rehna,
Meri har harkat pe,
Yuhi tum nazar gheri karke takhte rehna,
Jaise Meri har nayi silayi dress ke trial waqt,
Yuhi tum sehlate rehna
meri zulfo ko har aandhi se bachate rehna,
Yuhi tum bekhauf kamre me chale ana,
Meri sari gardisho ko alag daire me rakh ke,
Meri har ahem mulakato ko mathe pe tum chum ke apni ardas
sath rakhna,
Yuhi tum khatkatate rehna
Mere dil ki jagah aur bhi gherati jayengi,
Tum bus apni baho me mujhe simat ke rakhna,
Sare gum tumhare mai bhula dungi;
Tum sirf tum bane rehna,
Tum sirf tum bane rehna,
Meri sari kahani wahi tham jayengi,

Meri sari kahani wahi tham jayengi.
- Oshin Shahare

Oshin Shahare

I m a 23 yr old young, budding architect n adventurous soul from "City of oranges" (Nagpur) thats how I like to keep my city and my dreams simple,sweet yet a pinch of sourness in life.Just when things go wrong and feelings apart, take a deep breath, open ig n search on to my profile @theunuttered_words__ . Feel free to visit us with a cup of coffee in one hand maybe.

22. That's My Heaven

So when the people are nice,
Life's full of sweet and spice,
People around you are wise,
There's the time for you to raise!
That's my heaven.
When you live for yourself,
When you care little less.
When you don't hold your breath,
For your most favourite dress.
That's my heaven.
When your terms are clear,
And You state them to all,
And you really find someone,
Who'll never let you fall.
That's my heaven.
When you get touch of nature,
And you pet your loved pet,
When you stand for something good,
And you win that bet.
That's my heaven.
When you meet your friends,
It's long time since,

And you talk for hours,
Also confessing sins.
That's my heaven.
When the breeze is cold,
But you have someone warm,
Having good hot coffee,
Makes it beautiful and calm.
That's my heaven.
When you make something by yourself,
Your inputs make deposits,
No matter what's the outcome,
You are happy even in opposites.
That's my heaven.
Stuffing your tummy with goodness,
More than space in your heart,
Praying to god the only thing,
Till loss of appetite makes us apart.
That's my heaven.
When dreamland is conquered,
And you become the dictator,
That's when you're consumed in,
And sleep becomes the predator.
That's my heaven.
-Needhi Deshmukh

Needhi Deshmukh

Hey! I'm Needhi Deshmukh '21.

I'm a final year engineering student at YCCE. An enigmatic yet rationally tranquil writer who uses poems to funnel imagination and thoughts. It has always helped me in rousing when grief or self-doubt pins me down (sometimes withouta point). BTW, do you know where the poets come from?.....poe-tree. Sorry ;)

You can follow me on @quotes_scintella on Instagram. I hope my poems bring charisma to your day.

23. Beshaq Wo Behtar The

Tute huye dilo se to wo chile huye ghutne kahi behtar the
wo bachpan k din is jamane se to kahi behtar the!
har roj tha milna yaaro se bekhauf guzarna bazaro se
kam hi the dost us daur me lekin behtar the wo hazaro se!
kabhi khudko ko bhi aaine me muskurata hua dekhna
kabhi gusse me wo toote huye khilauno ko fekna!
un khoyi huyi chizo ka khayal sab kuch yaad dilata hai
na jane kab badalta hai manzar aur kab bachpan kho jata hai!
wo bachpan ki shaam k lamhe dil ko pyaare hai!
ab to jindagi k din bas intezaar me hi guzare hai!
ye bechain si raaton se to wo shaam k lamhe kahi behtar the
wo bachpan k din is Jamane se to kahi behtar the!
- Lavish Rathour

Lavish Rathour

Lavish Rathour' 23. I'm a usual IT Professional with an, unusual and exceptional passion for Poetry, Shayaris and Ghazals. While mesmerizing and soothing ghazals by Ahmad Faraz, Gulzar, Kaif Azmi (to name a few), help me find the inner peace and motivation to keep going at every situation, writing shayari's dig up the real-me to the surface of my encapsulated heart and to elaborately explain my thoughts and opinions. The words I weave into the yarn of emotions are a souvenir for all the wonderful people and memories that's worth the world and precious to me. To have a better discussion on our common interests follow me @the_lost soul on Instagram.

24. Sadagi Zindagi Ki

Yeh duniya ke chaka-chuand dikhave nhi,
Ha magar,
Gharo mein khilkhilati hui hasi pasand hai.
Aaj paas mein lakhon nhi, ha magar,
Apni mahenat se kamaye 100 rs par bhi
ghamand hai.
Diamond ring ki khawaish nhi, Ha magar,
barely wale bade jhumke bhot pasand hai.
Starbucks ki coffee ki aas to nhi,ha magar,
Nukkad ki kadakedar chai bahut pasand
hai.
Mahenga mobile saath to nhi, ha magar,
Khude kamai ka purana cellphone bhi
pasand hai.
Khudki do pahiya nhi, ha magar
bus ki window seat bahut pasand hai.
Yeh na samjho ki ,ye zindagi samjote ki hai.
Muje sadagi se bhari zindagi bitana
pasand hai.
- Shirin Shaikh

Shirin Shaikh

I am a girl who loves reading and writing.being a nerd I have always been in my own world ,but writings keeps me attached to outer world as well. ;-)

25. Ye Kaha Kho Gaye Hum

Ye kaha kho gaye hum
Sunno Tumhare ho gaye hum
Sambhalkar rakha tha jo
Wo dil de diya tumhe
Pyar ho gaya hai tumse chalo ye keh diya tumhe
Bhala kabtak chupate apni mohabbat ko
Aur bhala kyu na bayaan karte apni chaahat ko
Bohot rokha khudko magar intehaan ho gayi thi intezaar ki
Nikalti ja rahi thi rut pyar ki
Khair pyar barsat k mausam may hi ho zaroori nhi
Magar ye jo bunde barasti hai lagta hai bunde bankar tum
baras rahe ho
Ye jo thandi fizaaye chalti hai lagta hai jaise tum mujhe chu
rahe ho
Mujhe wo kadak chai ek hi pyale se peeni hai tumhare sath
Ye mausam kya hai mujhe to zindagi jeeni hai tumhare sath
Tumhari aankho may ek alag sa nasha hai
Jisme mai kho jaaya karti hu
Tumhari wo khubsurat tasveere dekhe bina neend nahi aati
Unhe dekh fir takiye se lipatkar so jaya karti hu

Meri muskurahat ki wajah ab tumhari muskurahat hai
Shok nahi hai koe mujhe
Ek bas tumhari aadat hai
Fulo sa mehekta chehra tumhara
Batao zara koe raaz gehra tumhara
Tumhare har raaz ko apna raaz banaungi
Mai kalam ek sadharan si
Tumhare apni nazmo ka kaagaz banaungi
Tumhara khyal aate hi likhne baith jati hu aur ek kavita bann
jati hai
Kahani hum dono ki shuru bhi nahi hui magar meri kitab may
firbhi iski ek dastaan bann jaati hai
Rahat si mil jaati hai jb deedar tumhara ho jata hai
Aur mujhe dekh jab palke jhukate ho tum
Tumse ishq mujhe beshumaar ho jata hai
Mai nahi janti ki tum mere bareme sochte ho ya nahi
Magar maine tumhare alava kisike bareme socha hi nahi
Talash khatam ho gayi meri tumpr
Tumhare baad maine kisiko khoja hi nahi.
- Sakshi Mahajan

26. Ab Befikar Hokar Hi Jeena Hai

Haalato se haarti

Magar lab se muskurati

Aankho may nami

Isliye palke mai jhukati

Waqif hu girne se

Baar baar zameen ko chuti

Aasman may udne ka khwab dekhti

Par kat jaane se mai darti

Ummed lekr chal padi mai

Mazil aage dikh gayi

Raasta tha kaato se bhara

Nange paav mai chaldi

Hath thama kisine mera

Hausla zara diya mujhe

Udi mai befikar hokar

Tabhi achanak gira diya mujhe

Darr tha jiss baat ka ...wahi baat hui

Ujala chinn gaya mera

Fir andheri raat hui

Haari nahi mai

Khudko sambhale rakha
Aag thi jo andar mere
Usse se maine ujala kiya
Kaaton ki raah par phool bichaye kadam aage badhati rahi
Dhere dhere manzil meri kareeb mere aati rahi
Thaki mai zarasi
Baithi aahista se
Fir dekha aage to mazil aur durr nazar aayi
Fir samjha ke ab rukhna nahi hai
Chalte hai jana
Thakna nahi hai
Udna hai , ab girna nahi hai
Samete rakhna hai khudko ab bikharna nahi hai
Aur fir ussi raste par nikal padi mai
Jaldi nahi manzil paane ki
Ab zara maza safar ka bhi Lena hai
Darte darte jeeli ye zindagi ab tak
Ab befikar hokr hi jeena hai.
- Sakshi Mahajan

Sakshi Mahajan

I'm Sakshi Mahajan nd I'm 22 year old from Nagpur. I write poetries it's not my hobby bt I'm in love with this Poetry connects me with people glad that people Relate it with their life. I write what I feel and Poetry is something that gives me peace, happiness, nd love from people which motivates me to write more. This is the best way to tell people about your life nd your thoughts regarding love, life, and a lot of things. you can't learn how to write poetry. but yes you can learn a lot from it. If u ever wanna listen or read my words u can check out my writeups here:- @sakshimahajan

27. If Tears Had Colour

"Before you say, "Show some valour!",
Let me ask you if tears had colour,
Like a shade of burnt red,
And they were 'bled' and not 'shed',
Do you think they were cared about?
As colourless isn't disturbing to you, I doubt.
Would you call it water then?
Would you still ask me to explain?
You go, "Why do you have to cry?",
Because hey, it comes, I don't call it or try!
Maybe then, I would fail at hiding,
Behind my big glasses after I'm done wiping,
As stains would remain,
And I would no more lie about my beloved pain,
Maybe then you would kiss my eyes like a wound,
And to melancholy my breaths mightn't be tuned.
Now that I voiced you this version,
Will you please unlock me from this prison,
In which I wither without a wrong done,
Promising me, to remember tears aren't for fun?".

- Anuksha Arge

Anuksha Arge

I'm 20 and pursuing Bachelors in Physiotherapy from VSPM College. Above all that I love, like doing theatre, writing and performing poetry, reading. dancing. photography, painting, traveling, I love living life to the fullest , most! I believe that our lives are incomplete without love and purpose. Meraki is close to my heart and so, it is my purpose to help it grow and inspire talents and to provide them the value they deserve.

*To read more of my poetry @_theanuquoted_ _@annukshaaa_*

28. A Little Bit Like Magic!

A little bit like magic!
The way her eyes shine
When she writes
Under the night sky
Full of stars and moonlight.
Her eyes are like
A book
And she has a habit of hiding
Poems and stories
Between its pages.
She's the whole damn ocean,
While chasing
You find yourself lost
Somewhere
Deep inside.
A wall full of arts
She's the painting,
You keep looking for hours,
Not because it's so beautiful,
Because it has a story

That speaks to your soul.
She never runs away from her pain
She accepts her pain
And turns that into an art.
She's not flower
That easily gets burned in the wood fire,
She's the wildflower
That blooms after the wood fire
With the traces of different coloured
Flames in her eyes.
She's not a kind of girl
Who wants you take her pictures,
She's different,
She wants you to draw her
And add different colours from your mind
And pour some love from your heart.
She's made of moonlight
And stardust
Even darkness becomes beautiful place
Only by her touch.
A little bit like magic!
- Priya Vaswani

Priya Vaswani

Hii! I am Priya V. Vaswani. I am from the city of Oranges - Nagpur.I have completed my graduation and post graduation in pharma field and am working for Clinical Research Industry. I write my heart out!

Little happenings of my life turned into poetry

You can keep an eye on my writings at my Instagram handle - @pandawrites14

29. Patang Ya Parinda

Dharti chune ya aasman
Faisla hai ye mushkil
Beej bhi boye hain mehenat ke
Aur uchaiyan bhi ki hai haasil
Aazadi ki bhi khwahish hai
Magar dar hai astitva kho dene ka
Kuch alag banne ke sapno ke tale
Jindagi bhar aparichit hone ka
Mn patang hai mera ya parinda hai
Chahiye mujhe pankh ya chahiye manjha
Pr bin hawa to kuch n hoga
Khud se hausla hi karna hoga sanjha
Band nahi hun pinjre me mai
Pr lagta hai ek aangan ki hun panchi
Udna hai ab dur kahin pr
Lekin faislon ke bediyon me hun uljhi
Jude rehna hai mujhe apni jadon se
Pr aasman hai meri manzil
Samvridhi hi hai ekmatr rasta
Taaki ho sake vo kad haasil
- Mrudani Deosthali

Mrudani Deosthali

I'm Mrudani Mohan Deosthali a 20 year old engineering student from Nagpur. 'To express' is something I have always believed in, and what's better than reliving your thoughts through your own work. As they say "We write to taste life twice, in the moment and in retrospect."

30. A Dream Of Love

*The moon insist to fall asleep in her thoughts , But she became a
sunset and the weather was hot.
A flower in the garden blossoms a while ,
They took a moment and make her smile.
The mystery in her eyes have stories to tell ,
The moon rise in a day and sun shine in a night.
My words were drowning in her eyes , she became a seashore and
I was a poet inside.
A poetry of you fly high in air ,
You became my love and that's so fair.
A silence in our heart became a rhyming song, She was my
dream and our love was strong.*
- Sagar Ghotekar

Sagar Ghotekar

I am Sagar Ghotekar (The Mumbai's Boy-SGR). Basically I'm 20 year old young poet from Nagpur,Maharashtra. I'm Author of 'A Day In a Mumbai' Which is available on Amazon.I'm writing since two years and still improving and exploring the world with my poetry. For more you can find me on instagram @sagar.ghotekar_sgr , @sgr.poetry ,You can also Subscribe my YouTube channel : SGR poetry

31. Illusion !

Sometimes keeping quite is more difficult than saying it loud ,
Do we always have to follow the crowd ?
Levitating the compromises by us
Finding flaws to others ,
Is that even a reason to be so proud ?
To the genZ we all say ,
We all are independent in our life's in some ways.
Dependency is a fact so far,
Even Arjuna had Krishna to fight in long run in the deep dark !
So can we stop judeing people here and now ,
Let's just try to be sunshine to the nightfall people facing someday
somehow.
- Snehal Meshram

Snehal Meshram

Hey there , I am snehal Meshram. A Budding medico and a writer in my early 20's exploring different shades of life . Words give me sense of satisfaction and power to express what I could never anyways !! Sending you some of me !! Love and regards Snehal

32. Yaadein

Tum mujhe samandar se lagte ho.Tumhe dekhkar mai usme dub jati hu, khudko bhul jati hu.Teri ankhon ki gehrai me khudko itna kho deti hu ki mujhe is duniya ki khabr tak nhi rehti, na hi kisiki parvah rehti hai.Lekin shyd mai jisse pyar smjti thi vo bs ek chaht ho, kyunki mujhe lgta hai jo mohabbat aapko etna tod dale, khudse dur krde or bich safar me hi aapka hath chord de, vo mohabbat kaisi ! Par jo bhi ho, tumhare sath bitaya hua har pal mujhe yad hai.Kaise ham kisi ke sath bacche ban jate hai or kaise hame choti choti bat affect krti hai.Mai tumhare sath, tumhare gati se behne lagi thi, bhul gyi thi ki meri disha alg hai !Tum or mai to us do nadiyo ki tarah hai jinka sangam to ho jata hai lekin aage se unko alag alag behna pdta hai, or unki destiny matalab unka samandar alag hota hai ! Tum to uss sangam se ab kafi dur nikl gye ho or shayd apne samandar se mil bhi chuke ho or mai apni rah dhund rhi hu, apne bahav se ek naya rasta banate huye. Apne samandar se kab milungi mujhe nhi pta, na hi mujhe ab uski chah hai kyuki mai apne bahav me khush hu.Apne is naye safar ka har ek panna mujhe khud ke hatho se likhna hai. Is kahani ke panno pe na tere liye kuch gile shikve honge na hi narajagi lekin tumhari yadein hamesha mere sath rahegi. HAMESHA!

- Mayuri Kukade

Mayuri Kukade

I'm strong independent women with ambitions. I want people happy and relatable with my writing.

33. A Promise Of Forever

He wants to be my forever.
But I lost him for forever.
At first, we were good friends.
We never wanted it to end.
But as we all know, nothing is forever.
And I lost him for forever.
We haven't spent a lot of time together.
But still we shared a beautiful bond.
We met just for few times.
And become each other's special ones.
We used to chit chat a lot.
Sometimes on snapchat.
Or sometimes over a call.
And slowly slowly we fall.
Yes, we fell in love.
In love with each other.
From strangers to each other's heart beat.
Both of us were food freaks.
We discussed each and everything.
From career options to romantic things.
We were like a perfect couple.
We were not having any kind of troubles.

He even waited for me for few hours.
We virtually slept in each other's arms.
Having a long distance is not the toughest task.
Only, if you both want to keep it till last.
Promises were made to stay with each other.
To love and trust one another.
But you know what, promises are meant to be broken.
So many things were left unspoken.
Because as we all know, nothing is FOREVER.
Hence, I lost him for FOREVER.
- Gurpreet Kaur

Gurpreet Kaur

I am ambivert and pluviophile and an engineer. I love to write ,sing, and act.

34. Revel

Life is all about finding happiness in every thing that you do. When you are not seeking anything, it will find its way to you. Happiness is also a way to find what you are looking for within your present life. Love is in the little things of life. Find delight in small things and they will continue to grow. Sometimes you find exactly what you were looking for before you even realised you were looking for it. Embrace the good things in the present instead of trying to think about the pain in life. Find happiness in discovering what makes your soul beautiful.

Do not miss out on something that could be perfect just as it could also be difficult. Follow your soul. It knows the way. Keep your heart free from distress. Letting go sets down the pain and allows you to move forward in life without that pain to hold you anymore. Seek happiness, not perfect things.
You find yourself again, as when you do, you are going to embrace who you see. You have the chance to choose what purposeful you will do today, even if you have some problems. There's a lot that goes right in life. Look beyond the flaws, under the pain, through the past and into the capability. Sometimes all we need in life are little, blissful things. It is the happy things that get us through the

day. Take a step back and look at your life with love every now and then. You will be able to find just enough hope, happiness to get through the difficulties. No matter how difficult things are, there's always something blissful to keep us going forward.

- *Roopal Arora*

35. Stead

Life is meant to beckon you forward along the path intended for you. Thoughts arise to show you something about yourself and your life. It means something blissful is waiting for you. You have lost sight of what you really want. It's an opportunity to stimulate your curiosity. It gives you a chance to connect with yourself. Follow your heart and discover what matters most to you. The harder we fight the way we are feeling, the harder it is to feel that way. Accept what is, let go of what was and have hope in what will be. Feeling lost isn't meant to stop you in your tracks.

Feeling uncertain and lost is part of your path. See what those thoughts are showing you and embrace it. Not until we are lost do we begin to understand ourselves. If you don't like where you are, move. Falling is what makes us grow, it makes us stronger and more resilient. Thoughts can heal you.

Do not be afraid to lose yourself. Think about what you want to do with your life. Change happens in uncertainty. It means shifting into something different and letting go some things. When life isn't going your way, you have created the problem. You are also the solution. You become what you think. You will never be able to fix your life until you accept it is broken. Find something you are great at and become perfect at it, you will feel passionate about it. When you know who you are, what you want, where you are going then nobody can stop you.

- Roopal Arora

Roopal Arora

Roopal Arora. She has done engineering in Information Technology. She has done Masters in Business Administration in Information Technology. She is OCP and SAP professional. She is Microsoft educator, buncee educator and wakelet educator. She is a brainmaths professional. She has 6 years experience in big IT firms like Wipro and CNEB network as IT professional.

36. Little Women

A timeless tale of hardships and adventure,
Of ambition, curiosity and womanhood,
A timeless tale of March sisters,
rich with colours of joy, love and care.
A timeless tale of charm and innocence,
Depicting every woman's life,
her world of dreams,
her flaws and strengths,
her beauty and grace.
A timeless tale of every Meg,
Pretty, romantic, sweet-natured and dutiful,
Unrealistically good and proper,
Who sacrifices her wish of,
luxurious married life,
for love of her life.
A timeless tale of every Beth,
an angel of every house,
too shy to go out in the world,
happy with her family, pet-cats and dolls,
with earthly love for music and singing,
and an eternal muse for her sister.
A timeless tale of every Amy,

A pretty child that turns out to be
a stately woman, with blue eyes
and lovely golden hair,
with grace and politeness,
an amazing artist adored for
her classy behavior,
but always anxious about,
her appearance and bodily features.
A timeless tale of every Jo,
a clumsy, blunt, opinionated and jolly woman,
ambitious and fierce,
to be found in a corner of attic,
absorbed in a book,
who believes that ,
women don't just have minds, beauty and souls,
they have ambition and talent as well,
they are not just meant for love ,
or getting married.
A timeless tale of every meg, beth, amy and jo,
a tale about how societal cliché's,
shape every girl's life,
about how the ones like our four little women,
flows against the flow of river ,
and define their life to the
stereotypical mindsets and patriarchy.
It's a timeless tale,
To be repeated on and on,

To each generation of women,
For how love, loyalty, ambition,
talent, independence and strength,
go well hand in hand ,
with no fear of storms,
for they'll learn to sail their ships.
- Prarthana Paunikar

Prarthana Paunikar

I am Prarthana Paunikar from Nagpur, Maharashtra.
Everything in this cosmos interests me but Nature and it's
conservation is my first love. And performing arts especially
Dance is what I am good at.

37. Wo Ladki Hasti Rehni Chahiye

Uski aane ki aahat se bhi dil hasta hai
Uski aankho me jaise noor basta hai
Uski maujoodgi me ik baat si hai
Uski nazdeeki meethi Barsaat si hai
Uska hona ek savera sa
Aur na maujoodgi ek raat si hai

Uska nakhra mujhse sambhala nhi jaata
Uska kehna mujhse taala nhi jaata
Uska bus gale lag jaana Ghar lagta hai
Uski khamoshi se he dar lagta hai
Uski muskan pe dil waar sakta hoon
Uski khushi ke liye sab kuch haar sakta hoon Aur
Chaha na iske siwa kuch
Ki chehre pr uske wo hasi jachti rehni chahiye
Bhagwan wo ladki u he hasti rehni chahiye
-Dev Bhardwaj

Shayari

Gunjti hai baatein uski yaadein bankar
kaano me aksar
Wo ladki mujhe sone nhi deti

Khood ho gye kisi aur ki
Lekin aaj bhi mujhe kisi aur ka hone nhi deti

Ki Barsaat me bhi pakad leti hai ansu mere

Ya Khuda
Jee bhar ke bhi
ye ladki mujhe rone nhi deti
-Dev Bhardwaj

Dev Bhardwaj

Dev Bhardwaj , here I am a student currently pursuing my Masters. I came from a small town chandrapur Known as black gold City of India. I like Observing small things happening around me an, I love enjoying my own company Writing poetry and shayari is my hobby. To know more about myself follow me on instagram @devbhardwaj.b

38. Udhedbun

Udhedbun

Udhedbun mey hu mey ki kise chunu mey

Shadi toh krni h pr umar bhar k liye kiska sath du mey

Ma kahti hey jodiyan toh upar se banke aati hey

Papa kehte hey jo hota hey kismat hoti hey

Bhai kehta hey samjhdar aur achhi Naukri wala toh ho

Behan kehti hey, didi thoda romantic toh ho aur apki ijjat krne wala bhi ho

Dadi kehti hey Parivar acha ho, toh dada kehte hey hamara naam uchha ho

Kaise udhedbun hai ye, kisko chunu mey?

Aur dost toh sapno ki duniya me ley jate hey

Apne sey upar dekhna, itna toh kamata hi ho

Tujhe shopping karata ho, gumata phirata ho, toh kabhi hume bhi dinner pr le jata ho

Tu aise banake rehana , aise karna , aise mat krna

Dekh har ki apni kahani hey

Par tu toh yarr ghar ki rani hey

Kya mil jayenge ye sab guun kisi ek hi insan me

Ise udhedbun mey hu mey ki kaise chunu mey?

Waise chuna tha maine bhi kabhi kisi ko

Sab bdya tha, koi kami hi najar nai aati thi

Sare pamane hil se gye the
Jaise wo rab ka ishara ho
Mujhe doobte ko kinara ho
Mano duniya badal si gyi ho
Sapne saj se gye ho.
Par ek hawa k jhokein ne mujhe jameen par utara
Chuna toh sirf maine tha, is bat ka ehsas kraya
Is bar mey hi nahi tum bhi toh mujhe chuno, phir kyu
udhedbun mey rhu mey?
- Varsha Garg

Varsha Garg

Hii I'm Varsha, I'm 26 years old, I'm living in Mahendragarh (Haryana), A writer not by profession but for expression.I love observing things and pen down when things hit me. Feel relaxed after sharing my feelings with my diary. This is for the second time I am working as a co-writer. You can follow me on instagram @garg_varshu

39. Discovering My Reflection

That first rain, after the dry spell.
Turned the colors vibrant, to my sense.
The start was beautiful as the stars.
As I walked through door of the hallway
I was amazed or puzzled, I can't say.
It was when I saw you, for the first time.
I couldn't look away from your beauty.
And your grace froze me like in a movie.
Your voice was soothing as the note of dawn.
The way you looked at me, with awe.
It felt like losing the cosmic law.
Your magic is like being enchanted by a song.
You took me to the horizon, you finish on my sentence.
A place you made in my soul, breaking all my defense.
I wonder how you are, just like my reflection.
And that is why love is beyond any explanation!
- Rohit Khobragade

Rohit Khobragade

I am Rohit, scattered writer since 2013. I started expressing my words after discovering what love is. I am an occasional singer and a guitarist with a music studio known as Synapsis production Studio. I believe in free world and free speech, and no one should stop expressing whatever they feel like, until its just words. In the end we get just one life. I am on the quest of wisdom, learning from perspectives, and love to interact with people. Hoping you all can related to the feelings in this short poem.

40. Aakhir kyu?

Aakhir kyu,mata pita ka pidha baccho ko dikhai nhi deta?
Aakhir kyu,jis pita ne tumhe sanskar diye,ek din tum unhe hi
sanskar ka path padhate ho?
Aakhir kyu,jis pita ne tapakti hui chhat par apna kurta rakh
kar tumhe bighne se bachaya,unhe hi tum ek din bighta hua
chhod dete ho?
aakhir kyu, Jiss pita ne apni ghadi bech kar tumhe iss duniya
me laaya,ek din tum unhe hi duniya se jaa okne ko kehkar
bejjat karte ho?
Aakhir kyu,jis maa ne tumhe chalna
sikhaya,ussi maa ko chalti raah par chhod dete ho?
Aakhir kyu,jiss maa ne tumhe 9 mahine apne kok me panha
diya,usse hi tum ek din 9 din k liye bhi rakhne k liye taiyar nhi
hote ho?
Aakhir kyu,jiss maa ne tumhe bolna sikhaya,ek din apni baato
se ussi ki bolti band kar dete ho?
Aakhir kyu,tumhe maa ka laadla ka tag accha nahi lgne lgta or
jodu ka gulam ka tag lagana chahte ho?
Aakhir kyu,tumhe maata pita ka dard naatak or biwi ka dard
dard lagne lgta hai?
Aakhir kyu,jiss maa ne tumhare bimar rahne par raatbhar

jaagkar nikale hai,kyu aaj usse hi tum bimar chhod dete ho?
Aakhir kyu,tumhe barso se sambhalne wale mata pita ko
chhodkar kuch din meethi meethi baate karne wale anjabi
jyada acche lagne lagte hai?
Aakhir kyu,jin maata pita ne tumhe itna kaabil banaya unhe
hi kyu tum old age home bhej dete ho?
- Rupali Jha

Rupali Jha

Hii!, I'm Rupali Jha from nagpur maharashtra. I'm an IT
student besides it . my hobby is travelling and writing whenever
I'm free , I write what I feel imaginations expectations in a page
as my writing skills are grow day by day. You can follow me on
Instagram @rjha_quotes

41. Intezaar Rahega

Kabhi sath chala karte the yahi,

Aaj ghumnaam se hai.

Kabhi raahi hua karte the yahi,

Aaj alag alag raah par hai..

Wo haste haste ek dusre ko sambhalna,

Ek dusre ki baato me kho jaana,

Chalte chalte lagta tha

Manjil ek hi hai,

Lekin sath to bass raah tk tha,

Mukam to alag alag tay karni hai.

Shayad kismat me nahi hamara milna,

Yaa fir tujhe hi manjur naa tha mera tujhse yuh roj milna.

Logo ki baato me aake jo tumne raah badli hai ,

Thoda sambhalkar jaana,girane wale jyada sath dene wale kam

hai.

Mai to tumhare liye duniya chhodne ko taiyar tha,

Lekin tumhe to duniya ke liye mujhe chhodna swikar tha.

Khair,ab jab khushi chunli hi thi tumne,

Mujhe akela yuh chhodna tay kar hi liya hai tumne,

To ab mubarak ho tumhe tumhari khushi,

Aise to kabhi yaad nahi karogi,

Par haa jab duniya ki niyat se wakif ho jao,
Tab aake dekhna fir yahi,
Yahi raah hogi,yahi manjil hogi,yahi mai rhuga,
Bass kami rahegi to bass tumhari,
Ho sake to aake puri kar dena ,intejaar rahega.
- Rupali Jha

42. Do Shakshiyat

Har insaan ke hote hai do pehlu
Do Shakshiyat,
Ek hai jo ladna janti hai,
Aur ek jise sirf pyar karna aata hai
Ek hai jo durson ka sahara banti hai,
Aur ek jise khud kisi Aashiyane ki talaash hoti hai.
Ek hai jo Samajhdaar hai,
Aur ek jisme sirf hai bachpana.
Ek hai jo chattano ki tarah majbut hai,
Aur ek phoolon ki tarah nazuk.
Ek hai jo duniya ka bojh uthaye,
Aur ek kisike kandhe par sir rakh kar apna haal bataye,
Ek hai jise rona nahi aata,
Aur ek jo dusron ko khush dekh kar muskuraye.
Ek hai jise kamyaab samjha jata hai.
Aur ek ko Nakara,
Ek hai jise bade aasani se log apna lete hai,
Aur ek ko kaiyo ne hai thukraya.
Har kisike hote hai yeh do Pehlu,
Har kisi me hoti hai yeh do shakshiyat,
And being a disabled person,
Mujhe dhyan se dekho

toh yeh do shakshiyat mere jism par bhi saaf saaf nazar aate hai,
Mere jism par bhi saaf saaf nazar aate hai.
-Nidhish Dikhit

Nidhish Dikhit

There always exist multiple Possibilities to get something done and make a change, And the best thing about being a Human is we are able to explore those possibilities and understand them. Human specie isn't made to be helpless. I'm a disabled person..and so i have a different perspective about the world we live in. It's been 21 years I'm living in this body and so I'm able to understand how's it like to be a human and what being capable or incapable means. I'm into philosophy (Stoicism)

43. Tere Na Hone Se Kuch Kammi Se Lagti Hai

Tere na hone se kuch kammi se lagti hai.
Hoto per muskan bhale kyu na ho
Mere palko me nammi se lgti hai
Bhedh me khadi ho bhi jau char logo k sath
Per dil me tanhai se palti hai
Tere na hone se kuch kami se lagti hai
Jab bhi dekhti hu aaine me ashk apna
Nazaro k samne aa jata hai, tere sath bitaya vo her ek lamha
Dhokha tha? Ya sach? Vo Jo bhi tha
Per mere dil ne tujzse sacha ishq kiya tha,
Majburiyo ka hawala de kr jab rishta tumne toda tha
Sach kahti hu jaan mere ruhh ne mano
Sharir ka sath choada tha
Khair, ab purani ho gye vo baate hai
Tere nazaro me shayad dhundhali ho gye hongi vo yaade hai
Per mere zahan me aaj bhi kuch baate chubha karti hai
Tere intazar me aaj bhi mere nazare rasta takka karti hai
Aur jaan tere na hone se kuch kammi se lagti hai.
- Swarnita Chichkhede

Swarnita Chichkhede

Iss badi se duniya me aapna chotasa aashiya banana chahti hu
Mai Jammi per rah Kar hi aasmano me udhna chahti hu.
Beshak daulat shouhrat Ki kammi ho zindagi me.koi. Gam na
honga Mai logo k dilo me aapni jagha banana chahti hu.

44. Ek din hum sab apni ghar ki tasveer le jayenge !

Chai ki chuski

Papa ki muski

Behen k sath ladaiyan

Mumma ki badhaiyan

Hostel jate wakt humein sab yaad ayenge

Ek tasveer hum sab apni ghar ki le jayenge

Ek tasveer hum sab apni ghar ki le jayenge!!

Kehne ko toh hostel bhi ek Ghar hoga

Par akele hone ka humesa dar hoga

Beshak vaha dost bhut milenge

Yaron me sayad hum vaha bhi khilenge.

Lekin...

Lekin lectures k bich mey "Apno ka call kiu nai aaya" yahi soch

satayenge

Ek tasveer hum sab apni ghar ki le jayenge

Ek tasveer hum sab apni ghar ki le jayenge!!

Bechaini jab bhi royenge hum vaha

Aasu pochne ke liye koi hoga kaha

Tab samajh ayegi

Hume akele jeena sikhna hoga

Apni kismat apne likhna hoga.
Par fir bhi
Par fir bhi wakt k uss dour me apno k kisse hum sabko
sunayenge
Ek tasveer hum sab apni ghar ki le jayenge
Ek tasveer hum sab apni ghar ki le jayenge!
- Avinashi Bhattarai

Avinashi Bhattarai

Jasbaat ko bas alfaaz me badalti hu! Duniya se thoda alag mai
chalti hu!

45. What I hide behind my poems?

What I hide behind my poems,
may be
the dynamic emotions
Oscillating from highs to lows
Sometimes aches of wounds
Hidden bruises on skin,
or odyssey to ecstasy
or mystery of perpetual beam
What I hide behind my poems
the craving to screech unsaid feelings,
Urge for screaming my throat out
voices eating me from inside
My poems make me able to avert
the vex and rage inside
Making everything flow on pages
Extricating my soul
What I hide behind my poems
Dreams I hid back in my closet
No, it weren't absurd and unfeasible
But I was coerced for undesired path

My poems bring me hope
to live those dreams at least in imagination
I hide the pain of being unheard and
My poems bury the hatchet which smashed my dreams
What I hide behind my poems
the overwhelming content moments
And weaknesses I try to embrace
the darkest times and happiest journeys
Unrequited love and my imaginary world
I hide the fragrance of the dried rose
I never gave to one I loved
I hide myself behind my poems
- Rajshri Chalakh

Rajshri Chalakh

I'm a lawyer and poetry enthusiast. She's all about her loved ones, books, food, sunflowers and poetry. She believes in being grateful for everything. She lives on a quote that says "Live for each second without hesitation - Elton John"

46. Ek Nazm

Voh aata hai bure waqt ke kat jaane ke baad
Sooraj aaya hai baadalon ke chhat jaane ke baad

Doshi ko faansi hui izzat lut jaane ke baad
Chaand ka kya kaam raat ke kat jaane ke baad

Yaad karte hai log logon ko mar jaane ke baad
Diye mein tel daalte hai lau ke mit jaane ke baad

Apne shohrat ka voh akela jashn manata
Maa baap ki yaad aayi usee sab lut jaane ke baad
- Rohan Iyer (aksar)

Rohan Iyer (aksar)

Engineer at dawn. Poet by dusk

47. "Ruin is a gift. Ruin is a road to transformation."

"Ruin is a gift. Ruin is a road to transformation."-Elizabeth Gilbert (Eat Pray Love)

These words relate to the situations so many of us come across in our lives. There are moments when we just lose hope and hold a firm belief that everything has come to a standstill, there is no way out of the crisis.
But there is somewhere the guiding light, that paves the way for us out of the tiring times.
All of us hit ground zero at some point.
All of us face a complete bleakness.
All of us have a low point in our lives.
It's at that time you witness a life changing moment or experience that makes you realise that in order to achive greater heights, you have to rise from the lowest point. You have to take risks and deal with what life sends in your way to be the better version of yourself.
- Manpreet Kaur

Manpreet Kaur

The author is Manpreit Kaur. She is a Post Graduate in English and qualified UGC NET. Presently preparing for her Phd. She belongs to Jammu but presently staying in Chandigarh. She has been a keen writer since school days as she started reading a lot. Writing is very crucial to her as it is the medium of purgation of her mind from the negativity that happens around. Along with this she is a music lover, a photographer who just wishes to capture everything around to make it an everlasting memory and a travel lover too because she is an Army kid and stagnation isn't something that she likes.

48. Lost in the wanderland

Lost in the midst of the wanderland,
Just me, clouds and the sand.
Suddenly a sense of inferiority troubles,
I'm just about to sunk but I was subtle.
I have been tormented by self-doubt,
Lamented but still want to shout.
Who knows what misty will happens on this wanderland,
DAMN!
This was dream & me having your peculiar hand.
She wakes me up on icy winter morning,
Just me, cold breeze & strengthen feeling.
But the breeze is blowing slow today,
Moving to a flat, tuneless landscape
Heart beating fast,
Hands shaking constantly and
My temperature risen up
Did something happened?
Home will be not home without you,
Because the energy has been lost now
I was so happy to get you,
Now you're leaving too
I'll miss you,

The things you taught and your kindness too
You taught me about self esteem,
But now I'm lost
Lost with so much optimism, enthusiasm
You gave me
I could write a book on you,
That's how magical you are
You came as god's grace,
That's gonna' stay in my soul
The ectastic smile of yours,
Is enough to make someone's day
I know you will be there by my side,
But your presence will be missed
Wish I could say you to stay,
Just want to see you happy everyday
I wanna' give you a crown,
even if I drown
I respect you so much
I owe you so much
I'm grateful that I met you!
- Srushti Lande

Srushti Lande

I'm an artist who's basically figuring out life. A writer, a photographer, a content creator, a human being who is basically contemplating while running a Youtube Channel, Instagram page, Spotify podcast and playlist, Quora and Twitter.

49. Tu Jarashi Ye Na , Aani Ithech Rahun Ja Na!

Haluvaar yee na!

Ithech rahun ja na!

Kadhi mala tu bghu de!

Kadhi tu Mala pahat ja na!

Tu jarashi ye na , aani ithech rahun ja na!

Jay-Veeru ch Nan!

Kokilecha gana!

Koni madhur swarat gata!

Tasa aapla nata!

Hya natyala tu japat ja na!

Tu jarashi ye na , aani ithech rahun ja na!

Mazi najar bagh na kiti parkhi!

Janu hiryala baghnarya joharya sarkhi!

Tasech mi tula bghitle g sakhi!

Janu khajina aala mazya lekhi!

Mg ashich tu Mala milat ja na!

Tu jarashi ye na , aani ithech rahun ja na!

Yanda pausachi chahul!

Tashe tuze Paul!

Tu yet ahes!

Tu aali ahes!
Jau nakos aata!

Mothya nashiban tu parat milali ahes!
Mazya kavitela asach arth tu det ja na!
Tu jarashi ye na , aani ithech rahun ja na!
Tu jarashi ye na , aani ithech rahun ja na!
- Prathmesh Bhure

Prathmesh Bhure

I'm Prathmesh Bhure , I'm an engineering student,a young mind with romantic and a sensitive heart. I write in all the three languages Marathi,Hindi,English. I started writing poems when he was in 5th std. My poems especially depict my feelings,my experiences and thoughts.

50. I Love You A Lot!

Every single night
I just want to hold you tight
Be lost in ur arms
As its most soothing there
Between Ur fingers and my palms
I just want to rush and experience
slowly the warmth of your breath
from tip of your toes
to the heaven through your head !
The aroma of your soul makes me pleased
as if u r only meant TO BE MINE
NO DOUBTS neither Denying!
The gillter of your eyes I falled for the glaze
the way they look at me makes me amazed!
I Just want to be yours and you to be mine !
I LOVE U ALOT
Is that okay and fine!
- Jeet Agrawal

Jeet Agrawal

I am a wanderlust Nyctophile, who loves to pen down his thoughts & feelings into words. I am the one who craves for calmness of night. The Moon soothes my soul. I am 22 years old budding poet from Nagpur.

51. Har Sham

Har sham jo aati ho mere khayalon mein.
Aah bhi jao kbhi mera hath thamb ne.
Laga kr gale tuhme batau ki tum ho kya mere liye.
Sunau tumhe meri dil ki baaten. aur batau tumhe ki dill mein
kyu ho tum mere.
Hai khi khubsurat chehre ass pss mere.
Phir bhi na jaane kyu thamb jata hu sirf tumpe.
Mangi h maine khi mannate. aur meri hr Mannat ka aakhri
lafz tum ho.
Naa jaane yesa kyu hota h...main leta hu saas kuch ht krr.jabh
tum ass pss na ho mere.
Har sham jo aati ho mere khayalon mein.
Aah bhi jao kbhi mera hath thamb ne.
- Gaurav Rewaskar

52. Fears – My Inner Demons

Standing there in the midst of darkness,
She closed her eyes shut.
Forcing herself to be surrounded by nothing but blackness,
Today, she decided to fight, no matter what.
The inner demons made her weak,
The same which besieged.
Letting her fears get unleashed,
Oh! the almighty, how can you let her weep.
Now, she questioned the existence of that supreme,
Who shook her faith in what she believed.
No one but the night to listen to her scream,
So, her sentiments were what she perceived.
Clenching her fists tight,
Breathing heavily and emotions so sincere.
Consoling herself to feel alright,
I beg the invincibility, to let her inquietude disappear.
The closed space choking her throat,
The paranoia grabbing her mind.
The same is advising her to write the note,
She kept waiting for her thoughts to get kind.

Still waiting for the light to emerge,
For it to wipe her tears.
The efforts leading to a verge,
Where she can defeat her fears.
- Lalan Chaudhari

Lalan Chaudhari

A BDS Intern with a zeal towards reading, writing and crafts.
A girl of 23, whom you can most likely find scrawling down
something in a corner of a hall full of people. A person who is all
agog about learning new things. There is no wonder that I am
someone to writing as a landlubber to sea. But also a firm
believer of, "When an unbridled love, nothing can stop you from

pursuing it." My works are reflection of the empathy I carry and my thoughts towards the world. Instagram - @idyllic_poet_97

53. Dear Crush

My blurred and double vision eyes
Your star like eyes
Whenever I see you my sadness dies
Your eyes are like a ocean
I think my heart is stolen
Your eyes use as celt
When you look into my eyes my heart get melts
Your childish behaviour
Makes my mind go crazy
And July is the season of rainy
Your pink lips
Your smile makes me cheerful
Your soft chubby cheeks
Dear crush you are beautiful

- Sujal Devidas Kotrunge

Sujal Devidas Kotrunge

I am sujal , 17 years old from nagpur. I recently started writing shayri's and poem, I am sharing one of my poem here whose name is 'dear crush' . This is my fantasy that there is one girl and i like her and want to tell her that she is beautiful. If you like my poem then follow me on insta @sujal.k_12

54. "How Poetry Saved Me"

I started writing for a cliche reason - to impress someone who was clearly beyond being impressed by me. With time, the purpose of me writing poems changed - sometimes for love, sometimes for the absence of it, and at times, just to be heard. Poetry never complained. Just kept coming.

1 AM scared of walking down relatively unknown roads, for the fear of getting lost. Doesn't applies when I start with a poem. Can't get lost when you don't know where're you off to.

To write a poem about something is much like lending that thing a heartbeat, along with which comes emotions, and subsequently, actions - which otherwise would go unnoticed, had a poet not written about it after falling in love with it. We fall in love with all things living, human - and poetry humanizes everything - it makes the sun rise and hide behind the horizon, sea waves calm or angry, wind a lover's breath (this, I borrowed), a diary a friend, and injects enough life into a corpse to stare right back at our vices, right through our clothes.

Poetry helps to forgive. And forget. To others, and when others don't forgive us, to self. And not just to the good guys. To anyone seeking forgiveness.

Lastly, (I'm just writing it towards the end, it actually shows up in every poem I've ever written) my poems never really had any depth in them - they begin with the foremost thought in my head which is largely rudimentary - and might progressively increase in depth as I think along. My poems never judged me for that. My poems never judged me for not being a good poet.

To say poetry saved me would be an understatement.
- Abhishek Jha

Abhishek Jha

I am a 25 year old MBA graduate who works at TATA AIG and thinks long and hard about getting his life in order during weekends.

55. To The Elder Brother, Everyone Must Have.

They say elder brothers can be bossy at times, can be irritating in some instances, can beat you for fun, and can make your existence difficult. But to be honest, brothers are a blessing in disguise, they will be the one who stands firm in front of you like a rock.

For me, it was always him. The one whom I had seen mimicking me very weirdly just to upset me, the one who used to make me smile wide as a kid, the one who used to take me on bicycle rides, who gave me the chance to bat while playing cricket, who used to run near the stairs just to make sure that I climb safely and also the one who used to wait upstairs to celebrate my 'first-time' climb.

From celebrating my little achievements to helping me select a career. From holding my hand as a baby to holding it during my teenage years, you made sure that I never feel left out. From telling Mumma- papa all my mischiefs as a baby to keeping my secrets safe with you, you've proved what a brother looks like.

I will never, ever be able to pen down what you mean to me, just know that you are my literal world. They say girls admire a person who protects them like their father, but for me, it will be someone who would protect me as you do. You are my superhero, my saviour. No matter how old we get, how far apart we stay, how many new relations we bond to, what we have is irreplaceable. You are my absolute best friend and secret keeper.
- Anisha Shirgaonkar

Anisha Shirgaonkar

Hii It's Anisha! I'm just a 19 year old girl who prefers books over humans and movies over the chaotic drama of life. Writing for me is literally an escape from everything. It allows you to engrave the dullness of life magnificently.

56. Greenery

Wherever there is greenery,
The scenic beauty is very beautiful,
There are lots of trees,
It refreshes our mind with positive thoughts.

Trees gives us enlightenment,
It provides us fresh air,
Where there are more trees there are more fragrance of flowers ,
It gives us energy and strength with relieving stress.
- Bitthel Agarwala

57. Feelings

When the feelings are very true,
No matter what happens,
The whole support of the world will be there,
No one can stop from getting it.
Whatever happens occurs with God's desire,
Without Him no leaves can move,
Whatever feelings comes under my heart and mind,
That is all what God desires.
- Bitthel Agarwala

Bitthel Agarwala

The writer is born and brought up in Malda, West Bengal. He is persuing BBA from SMIT,Sikkim. Writing, singing, creativity and Art is major interest field.He loves to learn about different cultures, travel and family.Looking forward to grow and develop along with the rural sector of society and bring out the hidden stories for the world.

58. Dreams

Don't let anything break your dreams
Don't forget them,
Get up ,run and don't stop until you accomplish them,
Don't stop until you get what you really wanted,
Get lost in the scent of those dreams.

Fall in love with the process of accomplishing them not just with
the thought of success,
Don't think too much about what's gonna happen just try to give
your best shot,
And even if you fail,
Try to find your mistake
And then learn from it,
But please don't stop until you accomplish all your dreams.
- Sakshi Jain

Sakshi Jain

Hey! So this is sakshi jain and i'm recently completed my B.tech and i love to write because i feel that we can simply write down the feelings that we can't share with anyone or the feelings that can't be understood and it calms me so much and gives me immense amount of joy.I believe that you don't only just have to follow your dreams you also have to fight for them. Trust in the process, learn from every mistake you do and carve your own path of life.

*IG: @ _shenu_writings_*

*FB: @ _shenu_writings_*

59. Hakikat Hai Ye Kahani Meri.

Main main Raat Bhar jagata Raha yah sochkar ki kal baat hogi
Gamoh ke kale badal chhae the mujhper socha nahi tha ki
khushiyon ki barsat hogi
Aur main manane aau to aau kaise
Tera naya shahar to jaanta hu magar Tera thikana Nahin
jaanta
Main Mahaj Teri ek tasvir ki pichhali diwaron se poochh kar
aaya hun makan Tera ,ab bus kar

main bhukha pyasa apni raaton ko jala kar aaya hun ,chhod
gussa ab baat Kar.
- *Kartik Bhalerao*

Kartik Bhalerao

" Mai woh hu jisne maut ko karib se dekha hai "

60. Tujhe Khone Ka darr Jab Likha

Tujhe khone ka jab darr likha

apni khamoshi ki shor ko zara mehsoos hone diya,

khamoshiyan bayan kar pana mushkil tha

jaise meri dhadkan ki shor ye keh rahi ho

ki tujhse mil pana shayad mukammal nahi ,

Ya maano jaise mere dil ka alam hi yun tha !

lekin fir khayal aya.

bichde hue parinde bhi to milte hongey na asmaan me kahin ?

Badal se boond girkar bhi to sama jata ha na usi samandar me

kahin ?

Fir ehsaas hua ki

ye zindagi ka pahiya ha

naa ki prakriti ka niyam !

yahan log milkar bhi faaslon ke kareeb ho jate hai,

Ya meelon door hokar bhi faaslon ka ehsaas nhi hone dete

tum to fir bhi iss duniya ki bhedh chaal me ek anjaan hi thehre !

umeed karna to door ab to khayal aane se bhi darta ha ki

tumhara naa hona kya kuch le jaega ?

meri zindagi ki berang tasweer ko kya ye rangon se saja payega ?
- Anchal Kumari

Anchal Kumari

Hey, beautiful people out there. I'm Anchal Kumari, an eighteen yr old girl just trying to figure out the way for her emotions and what they convey. I trust in the process of believing and improving myself, the only mantra to reach heights of success. I've been writing for the past 4 years and looking forward to going miles before I sleep.

ig - @aaannchal

twitter - @anchalkri

61. Hope

Rays of sun, will glitter in gloom,
Thunderstorms will end, flowers will bloom,
Chuckles will echo at the end of whine,
Darker the sky, brighter stars will shine,
Battles gonna end, victories will soar,

Wounds will heal, achievements will be more,
Tears will cease, smiles gonna unfurl,
Souls in melancholy, will sway and swirl,
Days of misery, sooner will end,

Caged rays of euphoria, will break out and extend
Clouds will pass, spreading brightness abound,
A heart carrying hopes, will outspread smiles all around.
- Srishti Pandey

Srishti Pandey

Hello readers I am Srishti and want to share my poems with you all. I have been writing poems for 10 years. Writing has always helped me to calm my mind. Whenever I observe something or listen something my brain just frames it down in words. Any expression or feeling can be beautifully presented through poems. Apart this I love to capture pictures and read books. Hope you all will show love to my poetries.

62. Remember or Forget

It's been ages since we parted our ways and yet I stay in dilemma
whether to Remember or to forget things that he presented me.
It was a bright Sunday afternoon
And as usual, my mood swings are at their peak
I was craving ice creams and whenever I have one
It reminds me of you getting me my favourite butterscotch.
My heart skips and travels to the era of love
Oh sorry!
Fake love that I lived and loved for a couple of ages
Wondering now if that could ever have been true.
I don't forget how restless your absence would make me
But I do remember how my eyes carried
the alarm clock of the entire universe
That would ring only by your presence.
I won't forget your love for fried fish over chicken
And magic moments over mountain dew
But I do remember how much you don't like Upma and idlis.
I won't forget you holding my hand every time I pass by
but I also do remember how senselessly you blocked me
Compensating the frustration over your ex.
I don't forget how every time you chose your friends over me
But I do remember how selflessly

I chose you over everything.
I don't forget how dumb
and stupid you made me feel
From your actions to all the presents that I ever gave.
I don't forget how effortlessly
I wanted to be the reason for your happiness
Despite you giving tons of reasons for sorrow.
I don't forget how hard I tried
to hold you back like the last string of rope
But I do remember how recklessly
you chose to be blind to all my efforts.
I don't forget that you dreamt of growing old with me
But I do remember how easily you left
Leaving everything unanswered.
I won't forget you questioning my love
But I do remember how you chose to play with my emotions
I won't forget you hurting me over and over
But I do remember it you doing For the sake of the comfort of
others
I won't forget you being my first but not last love
But I do remember how unworthy and helpless you made me feel
I wonder, If I should remember or forget
the time and the fake love that I lived once
But my heart weeps louder and asks
"Did you love to forget him someday?"

Then, I choose to remember and not to forget
Not only the memories but also the lessons
And today undesirably I am made of you and your lessons
And I promise I won't let the essence of your memories fade away

To all this, I set my heart ablaze
And burn the soul to ashes
Because they say to rise again
First, you gotta burn to ashes.
I wished to be a star shining for my moon
But then I remember that I burn like the sun.
And I know
Sun and Moon can't be together but they can be there for each
other.
And Now that I know I am the sun
I will burn and I will shine
Now that I know that I am the phoenix
I will rise again from the ashes
For, the time to burn has passed
And it's time to rise and shine again!!
- Shruthi Kasture

Shruthi Kasture

Kasture Shruthi, a Soul embedded with beads of love. She is a medico by profession and an artist by passion and forever a moon lover. She believes in the power of dreaming and achieving it finding her hope from the rays of the sun and blooming buds. She believes a star is still a star even if it fails to shine someday. Ig : @_d_selenophilic_writes

63. Laut Aao Na

Laut aao na
Ab likhte likhte thak gaya hu tumhare bare me
Choti choti khushiya dundh kar thak gaya hu dusro ke Sahare
me
Bhale hi ab hamara koi nata nahi hai.
Magar kya karu
Baat karte karte neend se Aakhe mundlu aise koi Sulata nahi
hai
Har raat isi baat ko soch soch kar dil bahal jaata hai ki kabhi to
aao gi Tum.

Laut aao na tumhare alawa dil ko koi bhata nahi hai , aisi
shidad se pyaar koi nibhata nahi hai
Roz uth te se ye Khayal aata hai ki ab Meri zindagi ki lakeer se
tumhara naam mit chuka hai
Ek hi galti ke pachtave ko bar bar dohrane ka kya matlab
Magar jab bhi tumhe roz dur se aate hue dekhta hu , dil man
ke darwaze par phir khat khatata hai
Rota hai chilata hai phir Bil bilbilata hai

Laut aao na , muh se nahi to kya hua mera dil apni sanso se tujhe roz bulata hai

Kabhi kabhi baithe baithe hi Teri yaadeyin mere Khayalo ke ghar me aisa ashiyana banati hai Mano saalo se wahi reh rahi ho.

Shaam ke us dhalte Suraj ko dekhte hue coffee pite pite Teri wo idhar udhar ki baato ki sudh mere man me tere sath bitae un palo ki aisi baad laati hai mano hum usme Abhi tak beh rahe ho

Aaj bhi raat me Meri neend wo sapne tod dete hai jaha Me tumhe aisi hi koi Kavita suna raha hu aur aur Tum has kar sharmane ki bajay mujhse milo dur jaa rahi ho , kisi aur ke thoda aur kareeb aa rahi ho , Wapis aaogi na puchne par na karte hue apna sir hila rahi ho me phir se puchta hu , kya Tum wapis aa rahi ho ?

Laut aao na mujhe chod kar kyo jaa rahi ho.

- Rachit Kothari

Rachit Kothari

As it is rightly said , "I have never started a poem whose end i knew . Writing a poem is discovering " ; and that is precisely what I hope to do everyday . I am a young 18 year old poet from Mumbai who loves poetry and literature . I have written several pieces besides this one and have performed it many times in open mics as well. If you wish to know more do visit my Instagram page : @thehuskyvoiceddude

64. If She Will Born

If she will born
I will teach her to embrace her scars rather than her beauty
For her to understand personality isn't all about looking tucked
in well enough but more about what you would bring to the
table.
There will be many bragging about money and materialistic but
only a few wanting to be a change.
I will teach her to be okay with her growing facial hairs and
remove only if she chose to not because her boyfriends ideal image
of a girlfriend doesn't match to her
I will tell her to not be trapped in the boxes and limits others
will set for her
I will tell her it's okay to like black more than pink and red
because my nails use to be painted black as well too when I were
her age.
I will tell her to be okay with being emotional and sensitive and
to feel emotions
After all emotions and feelings is a basic right everyone can have
then why to abandon her from the butterflies she will have
looking at that boy.
I will tell her to live freely but not foolishly.
*- **Khwahish_Nandini***

65. Panno Ka Sukoon

*Kehte hai shayaro ka ghar unke panno mein unki kalam mein
hota hai*

*Jaroori nahi har shayar aashiq hi ho kuch adhoore bhi hote hai
akele bhi hote hai*

Unke kisse kahaniyo mein kabhi tanhai mehsoos karke dekhna

*Kahi gumnami ke aehsaas bhi dhundhna dokho ki tabahi bhi
dekhna*

*Hum panno se aksar isiliye baatein kiya karte hai kyunki
duniya mein humein ghum dard baat kar sirf pachtawe hi
haath aaye hain.*

*Toh ab panno se aur kalam se kuch aisi dosti mohabbat karli ki
shayad jhoote rishto ki kacchi dor ki jaroorat na ho.*

*Humari khamoshi ki koi khaas wajah nahi hai bas kuch apni
hi galtiyon ko wapas na dohrane ka khauf humesha jinda sa
rehta hai zehen mein*

*Khwahish kisise rakhna pasand nahi karte ab kyunki chahato
ne sukoon se jyada bechaini aur dard hi diye hai.*

*Ab kisiko yea kisse sunane se behtar har din do lafz iss panne pe
utaar dete hai kam se kam koi bina bole sunne wala toh naseeb
mein hua.*

- Khwahish_Nandini

Khwahish_Nandini

Your reading Nandini, Khwahish_Nandini!
I m a literature student currently working. I belive in the power
of my voice and my words. I am also a fashion enthusiast, a
music lover and what not. I love exploring me and everything
else which excites me out of which poetry is one!

66. Anatomy Of Caskets

The anatomy of caskets

Tells us that

A 100 thousand years later

We all will have swollen ribs and broken noses with water

chestnuts at our feet.

We will long to go to an euphoria

Under the dogs feet

Who knows where the winds cross

To and the cheap Brandy liquor

In your armpits

Across the golden hour breast of a fallen dawn in the fall of my

eyelids

Without eyes. the feet barred

Over barbecued wires or troops

Of a forbidden season

In your backyard fire's suns

And shadows macabre around a forest fire.

A man walks in riddles and puddles

In the nearby pond

Split opening his mouth to procure carrots from Amsterdam And

apples from Bombay.

Leaving traces of his dust In the heat.

Leave your stifled fans
Outrageously original ovals
Of time fluctuations
In the atlas found on the Citizens of your tongue.
Breath in the morning
In the burned rosary
Of a dead grandmother
And a snowflake wedged between borders
Of Kashmir and Kashmir.

The anatomy of caskets
Tells us
That when a house burns,
Cross-stitch devices of string theories
On the palm of your hands
Click, click, click And tar varnished heels
In the corners of the circle That circle in infinity,
Vanish into a t(y)ear drop
At a light year of experience in handicappes
Of the things we lost in the fire, A fire that Ill(h)uminates Our
world in the dungeon.
- Sirisha Chauhan

Sirisha Chauhan

I am a girl, with the heart of hills and a mind of an ocean, both chaotic and calm coexisting in one plane. Well that's me Sirisha! I'm pursuing a degree in forest sciences and I love to read and write, in the laps of mother nature. You can catch me brooding, if I'm not busy or maybe just vibing to some random stuff in life! You can catch my work on @irisinawhisperr__

67. Kissa Tasveer Ka!

Kissa ye tasveer ka hai,

Ise dhyan se suno.

Vaado ki chadar.

Tasveer ke dhage se buno.

Ache lamhe bitaye jo,

Wo tasveer me kaid ho jate hai.

Jo guzare hai zindagi ki raho me,, Wo tasveer se yaad aate hai.

Kabhi khushi ka Izhar, Toh kabhi takrar ban jati hai

Ye tasveer hai mere dost,

Rishto ko aazmati hai.

Jab tak ho zinda,

Har ek pal jeelo.

Khushiyon ke jaam ko, Tasveer ke pyale me pilo.

Ye zindgi aaj hai ,

Kal nikal jayegi.

Har lamha, har yaad,

Ek tasveer ban jayegi.

- Amit Pandey

68. Dard!

Kya mehsus karoge is dard ko,
Jo dard muihe hua hai .
Meri ijazat ke bina,
Meri jism ko chua hai.
Dekh kar ye tamasha,
Zamana hairan hai.
Pal me rakh ho jaye,
Kya itni kimat ki jaan hai.

Kapdo ki nhi,
Baat hai saman ki.
Abhimaan se khilwad,
Kya itna aasan hai ?
Zakhm gehra hai ya ghau ka,
Jo meri ruh pe kiya hai.
Katra katra meri jaan ka,
Dard se yu siya hai.

- Amit Pandey

69. Online Ishq!

Ek online Mulaqat se dil bekarar ho gaya,
Na jane kab Koi anjane se yaar ho gaya!
Baatein hui; Raatein hui, lafzo me unse mulakate hui.
Na jane kab unka chehra dil ke paar ho gaya,
Ek haseen aadat si ban gaye wo, fur hume unse pyaar ho gaya!
Phir eh din jab izhaar hua, lak unki taraf se inkaar ho gaya.

Baato baato me wo keh gaye ki tum toh sirf dost ho, hume toh
kisi aur se pyaar ho gaya.
Ha dil tuta tha par hagigat se rubaru dil is baar ho gaya.
Mohobbat me phir ye dil zaar zaar hua.
Jiski muskurahat pe dil bekarar ho gaya,
"laj bhi Zehen me ek sawal hai.
Kya sahi tha main, ya mushe kisi galat se pyaar ho gaya?

- Amit Pandey

70. Duniya Mein Rehna Hai Toh Kaam Kar Pyaare!

Zindagi ke safar ki shuruaat kuch aise Hui, Aaye they duniya
me rote rote!
Badi si duniya mein lekar haath chote chote.
Na koi fikr, Na koi parvah, Na koi gam, Zindagi ki sachchai se
anjan they hum!
Ek din bada ho gaya zamana,
Rote rote hua school jana.
Karni padti thi padhai !
Jaise kitabo ke panno se ladai.
Phir bhi ! Haar nhi maani,
Kuch kar dikhane ki thi thaani!
Guzar gaya wo bhi Zamana, Ab pada college Jana.

College ka waqt bhi cool tha!
Phir laga! Isse acha toh sala school tha.
Itni padhai, itni taklife,
Likh diye panno par na jane kitne latife!
Khatm hua Sara taam jhaam,
Ab karna tha asli kaam!

Bas yahi zindagi ki dagar,
Takleef aur tajurbo ka ye adhbhut safar hai.
Is safar ko yuhi salam kar pyaare,
Duniya mein rehna hai toh kaam kar pyaare!

- Amit Pandey

71. Zindagi

Meri zindagi me aksar log shumar ho gaye,
Kuch aire gaire nathu khaire,
Kuch apne toh kuch parivar ho gaye.
Waqt aane par aazmaish hui rishto, Kuch logo ke liye hum
bekaar ho gaye.
Kuch ki baato me fun bane,
Kuch ki zindagi me funkar ban gaye.

Bohot Chand se chehre hai jinse mohobbat mili ha, Yuh toh har
lamhe me naftrat ke hagdar ban gaye.
Muskuraye hum, dosti ka haath badhaya,
Nibhayi dosti jab tak bas chala;
Phir Bhi na jane kaise hum gaddaar ban gaye.
Shayad nasee hi kharab hai ya kismat futi hai,
Ache bhale hum, zamane ke chakkar me bekar ban gaye.
- Amit Pandey

Amit Pandey

On the journey to find myself!

72. Khud Ko Pehchan Tu!

Suraj se pehle jag tu
Waqt ke aage bhag tu
Rakh hausale buland
Sine me lagale aag tu.

Jo rakhte nhi he wishwas tuz par
Bata de unko he sailab tu
Rakh mat dil me krodh - dvesh
De pyaar se sabko jawab tu.

Na dar mushkilo se
Bana lo khudko faulad tu
He aag tu , sailab tu
Khudki kabiliyat ko jara pehchan tu.

Na rakh ummid kisise
Apne karmo ko khuda man tu
Girgit he sb yha
Jara inko pehchan tu.
- Renuka Dehankar

Renuka Dehankar

Hii I'm Renuka Dehankar, I'm from Nagpur, Maharashtra. I'm an ordinary person who prefers to write extra-ordinarily.

73. Talash

Meri khayalo ki hey yeh kaise nazakat
Tere husna ki dekho yeh aise banavat.
Tere hoath jaise bheega samandar hey
Nighaye jaise kisi jheel ki sajavat.
Yeh meri kaise gumnam si talab hey
Jaha tujhe dekhne ko aakhe mere thakti nai.
Tujhe paaney ki yeh meri taalab kabhi mitati nai
Mera dil hey yeh samandar tere pyaar k liye rukha hua
Tujhe pane ki pyaas yeh mere aakho sey kabhi bhujti nai.
- Pratik Ugale

Pratik Ugale

Hello All I Am Pratik Ugale, I Love Writing Poems And Stories. Mostly the past held things in my life. A poet is firstly a person who is passionately in love with the language in which he feels his love, emotions and pain can be expressed in the best way. I am a 22 year Old young poet from akola maharastra re-living the moment's of past with help of my poetry and verses and helping people connect with it. For more of my writtings you can follow me on Instagram as Pratik__Ugale & The_Deep_Pen_Traitor

74. Aakhri Mulaqat

Abke bichde to sanam hichkiyaan na ayegi
Is viraan kamre aur titliyaan na ayegi
Kar gaye mumtaj to khair hai shahjahaan
Is maqbaren me ab khidkiyaan na ayegi.
Chaar diwaro me qaid ho saanse humari
In chaar diwaro me ab siskiyaan na ayegi
Jaa chuke hai door bohot door abke
Kabutar naa ayege chitthiyaa na ayegi.
Is qaifiyat ke chadar mein raat rojanaa ayegi
Aansu aayege khwab aayege yaad rojana ayegi
Le gaye chain o sukoon to mubaraq hon
Aankhe band hogi par nindiyaa na ayegi.
Tere jaate se hi andaaze lagaaye thy maine
Is shahar me ab bastiyaan naa aayegi
Basar kar rahi hai mahamari bhukmaari yahaan
Meri pyas naa bujhegi yaha nadiyaa na ayegi.
Ek tu hi thaa laazawaab yahaa
Ek tere hi mehfil ke thy nawaze hum
Ab fazar ki chai me woh chuskiyaa naa ayegi
Tu hi kar gayaa hai dil ko pathtar
Ab is pathtar ko aakaar dene mastiyaa na ayegi.

Ek jholaa hai jisme shikayate dher saari
Ab in maslo ko hal karne badi hastiyaan na ayegi
Ab raabtaa hai mera rab se rojanaa
Ab uske mere bich chand murtiyaan na ayegi.
Tu maange mujhe sazdo mein
Or paayen mujhe pardo me
Mai gaflat me jiu sadaa
Ab is rishte me or galat fahmiyaan na ayegi.
Liye kagaz ki naav hum
phirtein rahe samanddar me sada
Hum doob chukein hai
Hum ho chukein hai fanaah
Ab humei daraane or kastiyaan na ayegi.
Bichad kar kar gaye zameen ko banjar
Alfaz humare ho rahe phalsaphaan
Itrr si mahakati hain baatein humari
Ab is baghiche ko mahkaaane kaliya na ayegi.
Kaise deepak jalaye yahaan
Kaise khushiyaa manaayen yahaan
Eid aayegi to chaand na ayegaa
Diwaali aayegi ti chaandniyaan naa ayegi.

- Rangrez

Rangrez

Hii, I'm Rangrez (AKA) Rohan Gajbhiye all i want to tell you is that, if you can't raise your voice, pick up a pen and a blank piece of paper.

75. Jaroori Toh Nahi

Muskura rahe ho humme dhek kar , kya haal hai janab ka.
Mein registan ka kataa hun , tum phool ho gulab ka
Nasha chadh jata Hai tumhari tasvir ko hi dekh kar , jaise
mein koi sharabi or , tum koi katra ho sharab ka.
Yrr tu saal ki baaten karti hai , hafte mein mulakat nhi karti
Tu duniya ki baaten karti hai mujhe se pyar ki baat nahi
Chand Roz ki baaten karti
Har baar ki baat nhi karti
Waqt gujar ne ki baaten karti hai Mujh se sansar ki baat nhi
karti
Wo ladki duniya ki baaten karti hai mujh se pyar ki baat nhi
karti.

Ki tumse bichad kar ishq karne mein har baar jaaunga
Aaunga Kabhi apne shehar , tho phele apne ghar baar jaaunga
Yoon tho haar baar jit jata hoom mein meindane Jung mein
Per mein janta hoon Tujese mohabbat karunga tho mein haar
jaaunga.

Ye Jo Tum najrein jhuka Kar baat kar rahi ho , palake utha
Kar baat kar rahi ho , kadam theek Nahin rahe tumhare
jameen per , aaj aankhen Mila kar baat kar rahi ho,

aur yah tumhare badan per hothon ki nishaniyan kaisi ?
yah tumhare badan per hothon ki nishaniyan kaisi ?
sach batao yah tumhari hi lali hai ya phir Kisi aur se mulakat
kar rahi ho ?
Jo Tum ja rahi ho mujhe chhodkar sach batao koi majburi to
Nahin. ?
Tumne sach mein bataya na tumhare jaane ka Karan , koi baat
abhi adhuri to Nahin ?
Hum najdeek to Aaye the na theek se , hamari nazdikiyon Mein
koi duri to Nahin. ?
Aur tumhen Jana hi Hai to chali jao mere aansuon ka Karan
mat poochho.
Har baat tumhen bata dun ye jaruri to Nahin!

Main baitha rahunga Teri bahon Mein Tum hath fer dena mere
galon per
main tumhen 90स Mein lekar jaunga lagaunga gajra tere balon
per !
jab bhi main baat karunga Kisi aur ladki ki Tu Mera baat
pakad Lena ,
hum barishon Mein nange pair chalenge to Mera hath pakad
lena.

Jab kabhi bhi milane aana mujhse ChaalBaaz , Chalaki ,
dimag , Ghar per chhod aana laga dena unko dhandhe per
aur han jismon ki tamanna Nahin Hai mujhe bus Tum apna

sar Rakh dena mere kandhe per!

Ki Tu Nahin Hai meri zahan Mein , fir bhi Maine tujhe Apne khyalon Mein kahin ghumte Dekha Hai .
ki Tu Nahin Hai meri zahan Mein , fir bhi Maine tujhe Apne khyalon Mein kahin ghumte Dekha Hai
Ab mujhe maut bhi a jaaye to fark Nahin padega
Maine apni mohabbat ko Kisi aur ke galon per chumte Dekha Hai!

Tum sunti ho sirf gairon ka , tumhen awaaz lagana be matlab hai
Jis Gali Mein Tera Ghar Na ho , vahan gulab lagana be matlab hai!

- Ayush Mishra

Ayush Mishra

Hii I'm Ayush Mishra Basically Mein ek shayer hoon shayari sunaungaa apna kaam Karunga haan sahi soch rahi hai tu Tujhe aaj mein in panno mein badnam Karunga.

76. Prem Vimochan

Yakeenan behtar kavita na likh paayi,

Behtari likhawat mai aati lihaja

Jab likhawat ki prerna tum hote.

Duniya bhi gaur-chaav uss kavita ki padhti,

Jis kavita ka mulroop tum hote.

Aakhir har koi jheel si aankhe,

Unme Pahadon sa nishchay

Sheetal hawayo sa muskurana tumhara,

Aur ramniya iss kaya ke varnan ko udvigna hai.

Par bas itna kaise kaafi hota,

Agar kavita tum par likhti.

Tumse prem ka vimochan toh,

Nayi bhasha ka janm hai.

Har bhet toh pratishthit prem kahani ka sutrapat hai,

Har bhavna toh samudra ka veg hai,

Aur yeh kisse bhi toh,

Kisi amulya rachna ka paatth hai.

Jaise tumse voh baatien, ki ,

Amuman premiyon ki,

Voh sabhi baatien abhi shesh hai.

Agar shesh na hoti toh yakeenan

Mai ek behtar kavita likhti.

Agar mukhar premiyon tulya,
Yeh bhi kahani hoti,
Jisme parivarik pralay,
Mitra sangat ayvam apna vilay,
Sahit prem mai sangharsh
Ki sabhi baatien hoti,
Tab yakeenan yeh kavita behtar hoti.
- Mahek Triphati

77. Tumhari Agli Kavita

Tum agli kavita mujh par likhna,
Labon ki surkhi, aakhon ka kajal, bikhre baal,
Sabhi ka kathan karna,
Tumhari aakhon se dekhna chahti hu khudko.
Dekhna chahti hu, dekhte ho kya tum,
Jab tumhare ek nazar bhar ko,
Mai surkhiyon ke saath prayog krti hu,
Inhi aakhon mai kajal bhar leti hu,
Taaki tumhara aashray (unme) duniya dekh na sake,
Baal bhi toh bikher deti hu,
Ki bahane se hi sawar doge tum,
Ab in sab baaton par jab gaur karoge,
Toh kya agli kavita mujh par likhoge ?
Kya tum kavita ke saar mai meri jhalak dekhoge?
Gaur toh krte ho na jab sard mausam ke bahane,
Tumse jyada kareeb rehti hu ?
Aur zukam lagne par dur daud lagati hu?
Usha se gaane tumhare liye gungunati hu,
Balon mai phool bhi fir sajati hu.
Tumari nazar se mai atkheliya
Agar kavita ke tuk jaisi krti hu,
Toh kya tum inme chupe prem se prerna lena chahoge ?

Aur kya tum agli kavita mujh par likhoge ?
- Mahek Triphati

Mahek Triphati

Somebody that roots for a life full of faith and love. Trying to put the idea of love to words, hoping it acts like a navigation light for those who have lost their ways in the darkness which is the other side of love. I like to re-establish faith in all the humans i meet. Poetries are a way for me to put words that i could have said to people if i had enough words and all words were just expressed as i wanted to put them like how all of us want.

78. Hugging My Dad's Shirt For The Last Time

I have some old clothes of my dad

He is above the clouds which makes me sad

2-3 jeans 4-5 shirts that he always wanted me to wear

Never did,Because of embarrassment and stupid fear

As an introvert i always denied

No I'll look like a nerd, i always replied

Reading those books , you left on shelf

Wearing those extra long shirts and hugging myself

While mixing your body ouder with some salty water drops

People says it's tears that's never going to stop

From hugging you to hugging your jackets, things are changed.

Your body was burning and i was fire-fanged

This air feels like you are caressing my hair

I need you everytime, why are you not here

it's kind a journey i never imagined, never expected, not even wanted

Dad please come back, 'i said' you never responded

You always gave me everything without thinking about your own needs

But dad without you this new wound hurts and bleeds
The things that bothers me a lot is i never confessed you that you
are my first love
Everyone ditched me in every possible way and shove
that i always want you to set my frizzy hairs
To take care of me from wild stares
that i always want you to see my achievements
My life is going according to society's agreements
that i Don't want to leave you for a stupid boy
I want to sit on your shoulder and feel joy
that you are like my oxygen, Insulin, Melatonin, Estrogen,
Testosterone, Cholesterol
Every damn thing which essential for my body and soul
I have lots of regrets with lots of beautiful memories
This shirts are part of my most beautiful stories

I am burning this shirts End of the chapter, no remaining
threads
I don't want to imagine you because it reminds me that you are
dead
For a long time i waited
This smell of your clothes is fading and I'm intoxicated
Don't worry dad this is not the end
I can't handle the burden of emotions
Will Meet dad on the Mariana trench.
- Prachi Ajay Dhoke

79. Hume Zinda Rehne Do Aye Husnawalo

Nasamajh hai ye log saare
Par ye sama shikayat ka nahi
Tu gunaah kar sareaam bewafa
Mujhe haqq sharaarat ka nahi
Ishq-e-bagaawat ka silsila hai
Ab waqt hidaayat ka nahi
Tu samajh mere maalik
Ye daur sharafat ka nahi
Tum shafakat ke bukhe ab Shikast sambalo
Hame Zinda rehne do aye husna walo.

Khatawaar tum sahi Saza ka haqq hamara hai.
Tum karlo thoda sabar Uski adalat main milna dobara hai.
Waha jhuthh na bolna Harchiz ka hisaab hai
Lekin Bina dagabazi ke tumhara hua kaha guzara hai
Guzare main guzaar lo itni gairiyat ginwalo
Hame Zinda rehne do aye husna walo.
Hadd hogayi to mohhabat zaroorat ho jayegi
Hadd hogayi to chahat ibadat hojayegi
Bekhabar ho tum jazbato se

Hadd hogayi to nafrat fitrat hojayegi
Ab tum hamari hadd ka andaza lagalo
Hame Zinda rehne do aye husna walo.

Ab to kehte ho main Qubool hu to ye intazar kaisa
Mujhe chhune se inkaar kaisa
Meri jaan, hum to zindagi the na tumhari
Fir Pyaar jatao, mushkil-e-izhar kaisa
Agar sath reh na sako to dil se nikalo
Hame Zinda rehne do aye husna walo.

Hayeeee Tumse shabdo main hare
Hare hum chahat main bhi
Tumhare shahed se dare
Dare hai zeher ki Rahat se bhi
Tumhare huye to duniya se ladlenge
Ladhlenge khilaaf-e-inayat se bhi
Par tum to hamse kehgayi hathiyaar dalo
Hame Zinda rehne do aye husna walo.

Tumhare bin zindagi maut se baddtar
Zeher lage dava, dava lage shauk se baddtar
Tum ho to sab hai, Varna haqiqat meri lash se baddtar
Jaoge chhod ke to wajood mera sath le jana
Ba-wajood sanse leta ye jism, lash se baddtar
Khauf bhi kahe mere qabar se, ab to dafnaalo

Varna Hame Zinda rehne do aye husna walo.

Khubsurat, to tumhari aankhe hai Main sawarke kya karu?
Tumhe pasand hu main, aisi hi Sudhar ke kya karu?
Basayenge tumhare dil main apna Ghar
Tumhare raste se guzar se kya karu
Tum bhi kabhi guzar ke, darwaze khat khataaalo
Hame Zinda rehne do aye husna walo.
- Prachi Ajay Dhoke

80. Ek Arsa Hogaya Hai Muskuraye Huye

Halato ke hatho majbur hona gawara nahi

Mushkilo main iss tinke ka koi Sahara nahi

Dafnaye gaye hai meri mohabbat ke phul sare

Iss kaafir ke baag main bahara nahi

Aree hum to hai hi husna se chot khaye huye

Ab ek arsa hogaya hai muskuraye huye.

Naa aaye samajh baate meri, tu samjhane wala yaar bulana

Koi jhaak Naa paye khidki se teri, tu bin aakho wala pehredaar

bulana

Par hum hi to the vo tumhare pehro main Dafnaye huye

Ab ek arsa hogaya hai muskuraye huye.

Tumse mohabbat karne ki mujburi na thi

Wafa se daga ki manzuri na thi

Manzur to tha nishano ko mera ghayal hona

Par goli tere hatho se chalni zaroori na thi

Chalo mana hum khoon se sane ulfat main hai zakhm khaaye

huye

Khair... ek arsa hogaya hai muskuraye huye.

Tum bhi sunlo jumle mere zehere main bhigaye huye

Tum kaise bataoge gunaah tumhare chupaye huye
Aree aasuon se to patthar bhi pighal jata hai
Hum to khoon ke aasu hai tumhare rulaye huye.

Sitamgar ho to sataya karo
Bharosa kar har sitam hai khaye huye
Nazre jhuk gayi mehfil main teri
Najane kaise nazaare hai dikhaye huye
Hum to khushiyo ki mehfil sajate maut pe teri
Ab ek arsa hogaya hai muskuraye huye.
- Prachi Ajay Dhoke

81. Jism

Mujhe tumhare jism ke har zarre se pyaar hai
Lekin Bistar ki numaish se hargiz inkaar hai
Mujhe mohhabbat hai.
Tumhari muskaan se Jo kaano se sidha Dil main utarti hai
Ishq ke har raah se guzarti hai.
Tumhari ungliyo see jiski har silwato se tumne sirf mujhe
chhuaa ho
Nadani main kuchh kuchh shayad tumhe bhi huaaa ho.
Tumhare kadmo se jinki aahate mujhe baichain karti hai
Chalte chalte lambe din rain karti ha.
Tumhari baahe jinme Marne se mujhe aaj bhi shiqwaa nahi
Janta hu jine ka mujhe bhi salika nahi.
Tumhari aakhe jisme aasu dekhne se main darta hu
Gustaq hu main jo bewajah tumhe sataya karta hu.
Tumhari peshani jise chumke tumhari har shikanj Meri ho jaati
hai
Maut bhi mujhe pehle mile agar vo tum tak aati hai.
Har talaash rooh Tak nahi hoti
Tumhe chhune wale uss har aihsaas se mujhe mohhabbat hai.
Iss kaqar hai ki
Tumhare sine ko chhu ke
Dhakane mehsoos karta hu.

Tumhare hoto ko chhu ke
Mere liye huye har naam ko mehsoos karta hu.
Tumhari saanso ko chhu ke
Apni maut ka anjaam mehsoos karta hu.
- Prachi Ajay Dhoke

82. What If I'm Dying!

Hey I'm cancer patients I have only few days left to live my life
I have lots of friends
And everyone is close to my heart
What I wanna say is
I love to breathe!
I love to listen my heartbeats.

I am thankful to every second where I breathe where I saw you
Yes you!
I am really lucky to have you in my life
But I am not forever with you
I really wanted to spend my time with you
I wanna touch your face with my fingers
I wanna hug u tight.

I wanna make you realize....that how it feels when the oxytocin
blasts in brain
If am dying in 2 day then I want more days between this I want
day 1.1, day1.2, day1.3, day1.4 etc
What I want to say is I want to live more
Or if it's a last day of my life then I want you to be happy, not
like a crying guy who only stare everything like a nonliving

puppet
And after dying I don't wanna be an angel I wanna be star that
I could be a evidence of your happiness.
Your not so alive friend or girlfriend
- Prachi Ajay Dhoke

83. Stree

Ab sati na satyavaan ke sath jayegi
Na sita ki agni pariksha ki naubat aayegi
Naa banegi aurat kisi pe bojh
Dropati apni laaj khud hi bachayegi.
Stree phool hai to talvaar bhi
Stree Prem hai to fatkaar bhi
Jaha Hawas ke bhukho ki shikaar bani
Ye ladkiya kurukshetra Mai hathiyaar bani
Maaf karde to Isha hai.
Ghusse main kaali ki hai aakh sani
Aadishakti hai stree Bina stree ke purush bejaan hai
Mera pura bhrahmand hai vo jisne mujhe Diya jivandaan hai.

- Prachi Ajay Dhoke

84. Teri Jhuthi Mohhabat

Teri jhuthi mohabbat ka silsilaa, Aaj hi khatam hoga
Hisab -e- Ishq -e- bewafai ka har sitam hoga.
Tujhe de jo diya darja khuda ka
Bhul gayi kutto se ghee kaha hazm hoga.
Mera baap chilla udhhta hai kharocho se meri
Unhe kya pata tere ishq main kitna gehra zakhm hoga.
Tere Sato rang dekhe zalim
Sukr hai safed Mera kafan hoga.
- Prachi Ajay Dhoke

85. Dark Nights

Have you ever noticed? That the night sky has so many stars but everyone talks about the moon
Some people adore the moon some hate but stars are different they don't care who hates them they lustre without any guilt they know how to shine for the people who see them with watery eyes,old songs and a cigarette.
We all have some flaws and woe we always think about ourselves But the stars falls too , to fulfill a vow
I'm like that star I wanna shine for you I can fall to fulfill your wish.
Stay with me whole night because I can't see you in daylight.
- Prachi Ajay Dhoke

86. Nahi Jaata

Ameer karte hai baat mehnat ki par pathro pe koi sone nahi
jata
Sab sunte hai taklif, koi sunke takiye bighone nahi jata
Ye jo ghamand hai na vo do gaz duri ka hai meri jaan.
Ye jo Jeet ke baithe the duniya
Inki mazaar pe aaj koi rone nahi aata.
- Prachi Ajay Dhoke

87. Avantika

Duniya se chhupaya hua Raaz hoon
Main dab chuki awaaz hoon
Gumnum hu main bheed main
Main waqt se naraz hoon
Sabar ki Main Seema hoon
Krodh si apar hoon.
Nafrat ke iss daur main
Main ankaha sa pyaar hoon
Khushiyo main Anjali si
Dukh main antika hoon
Har halat mein apnaungi
Main Avantika hoon.

- Prachi Ajay Dhoke

88. Tu Na Sahi Paas Mere Mera Akelapan Hai

Teri Mohabbat se ubb Chuka mann hai

Zakhmi hu main, zakhmo se Sana badan hai

Faaslo ki itni chahat thi Teri

Ki nazdikhiya dafan hai

Tu na sahi paas mere

Mera akelapan hai.

Badi muddato ke baad palke galo se takrayi hai

Khush hu dilse par sath tanhayi hai

Ulfat ka pata nahi sirf mili bewafai hai

Utari thodi khumari par bacha thoda dewaanapan hai

Tu na sahi paas mere

Mera akelapan hai.

Chhalakte ashk dekh, maine tumhe hasaya hai

Rakib ki baho ne, uff kitna tarsaya hai,

Aasuo se aag lagake tumne bhi kya khoob fasaya hai.

Ishq ki chadar thi hamari, aaj safed rang ka kafan hai

Tu na sahi paas mere

Mera akelapan hai.

Bohot khubsurat falsafa tha meri bandagi ka

Kaafi hadd tak irada tha tujhse dilagi ka

Meri mazaar pe tum milne bhi na aaye
Mujhse to wafa ka wada tha zindagi ka
Halaki ab nafrat main bhigoya mera awarapan hai
Tu na sahi paas mere
Mera akelapan hai.
Nashe se nafrat ki aadat na thi
Dhuye se badalo ki aafat na thi
Mere maikhano main mehboob ki khurbat na thi
Khair mere maslo main bhi sazavaar Mera pagalpan hai
Tu na sahi paas mere
Mera akelapan hai.

- Prachi Ajay Dhoke

89. Ishara Kiya

Tumhe pata hai tumhare dhoke k baad maut si lagti hai
zindagi
lekin Jab logo ne humse pucha ,tumhe mehfuzz jagah kounsi
lagti hai maine tumhari baaho ke taraf Ishara Kiya.

Badaa Ajeeb ho jata hai jab kisi rishte main ghutan si hoti hai
lekin jab havaa ne puchhaa tumhe chupke se chhutaa koun hai
Maine tumhari Saaanso k taraf ishara kiya.

Andekhaa kar dete ho tum meri saari khoobsurat chize jaise koi
khoobi ho hi na mujhme lekin jab nazro ne puchhaa tumhe
pyaar se niharta koun hai
Maine tumhari Aakho ke taraf ishara kiya.

Mithaas khatam hogayi hai zindagi se
Baato main ab kadwahat lagti hai lekin jab muskurahat ne
puchaa tumhe alfazo se chumta koun hai
Maine tumhare Hoto ke taraf ishara kiya.

Galiya Anjaan hogayi hai jahase guzarte huye zamana gaya
anjaan hogayi hai shakshiyat meri vo shaks bhi baigana huaa
lekin jab sadakone pucha tumhari manzil kaha se hoke guzarti

hai
Maine tumhari Raho ke taraf ishara kiya.

Bohot naraz hu main khudse shayad tumne barbaad kardiya
hai
Chinn k taqdeer meri mujhe bezaar kardiya hai
lekin jab kismat ne pucha tumhari lakire kisse judi hai
Maine tumhare Haatho ke taraf ishara kiya.
- Prachi Ajay Dhoke

90. म Se

Matlab samjha nahi

Matlab ki baate hogi

म *se mohabbat* म *se munafa*

Fir bematlab matlabi firate hogi

Mere mehboob ki mehendi bhi aayi thi mere mayaar se

म *se mashuk ,* म *se maut*

Fir beshaq Shaqqi raate hogi.

- Prachi Ajay Dhoke

91. Dekha Hi Nahi

*Tune par jo kaat diye mere, Maine udd ke to kabhi dekha hi
nahi*
Tune toda kuchh iss qadar Maine Judd ke to dekha hi nahi.
Dekh teri khudgarzi ka anjaam magrur
Aage qabar hai, piche main aur mudke to tune dekha hi nahi.

- Prachi Ajay Dhoke

92. Meri Nigahon Se

Meri Nigahon se teri nazro ko bezaar hote huye dekha hai
Pehli dafa ishaaron se kisi ko shikaar hote huye dekha hai
Aabru jo sine se lagaye chalte the bazaaro main
Unhi ko be-hayayi ke hatho bekaraar hote huye dekha hai.

- Prachi Ajay Dhoke

93. Being Heartless In Darkness

Deep depth have dark darkness
Gave up on feelings I'm heartless
Losing my hopes
Doubting great scopes
I Want to hang till death
On a hook, I am tieing ropes
From exotic hips to silent lips
From frizzy hairs to scary eyes
I measuring my height
For my coffin's size.

- Prachi Ajay Dhoke

94. Kabil Nahi Chhoda

Vo baate karti thi aasman chhune ki
Uski har fizool ki hidayat ne,mujhe khudgarzi karne ke kabil
nahi chhoda
Pyaar ka paimana durr Tak nahi hai
Khauf itna ki darne ke kabil nahi chhoda
Ek mohbbat thi uski jine nahi deti thi
Ek bewafai jisne aaj Marne ke kaabil nahi chhoda.

- Prachi Ajay Dhoke

95. Mohro Ka Mohtaaj

Mohro ka mohtaaj sirf paiso se manta hai
Muft ka shor nahi, sikko ki khanak pehchanta hai
Ye khoon ka rishta fareb hai maa
Log rishte bhi unhise nibhate hai, jo rishta kharidna janta hai.

- Prachi Ajay Dhoke

96. Wehem

Badaa shauk tha mujhe meri masumiyat aazmane ka
Sochta tha insaniyat hi taur hai zamane ka
Main nikal padha kal Khali Jeb liye bazar me
Mera wehem hi durr hogaya izzat kamane ka.

- Prachi Ajay Dhoke

97. Kya Ho Tum Mere Liye

Vo jiski zara si naarazgi meri buri aadate chudwaade vo ho tum

Mussalsal mujhe jiski kami khalti hai vo khawahish ho tum

Vo jo meri pyaari si muskan hai uski wajah ho tum

Jise khone ke khayaal se main ghabraa jaati hu vo darr ho tum

Jiske hone se mera wajood hai vo asliyat ho tum

Jiska k har dam main mazaa hai vo nasha ho tum

Meri ungliya jise chumne ko raazi hai vo falak ho tum.

Meri mohabbat ki intehaan ho tum

Vo rang jo hawaa main milte hi dhool banjata hai vo rangin

samaa ho tum

Jise main lafzo me kabhi bayaan hi na kar paau vo chahat ho

tum

Main jis shakks se har dafa karna chahu vo mohabbat ho tum.

Main har dhoka bardaash karsakti hu lekin tumhari udaasi

nahi

Tumhari muskaan se badkar kabhi kuchh mere liye tha hi

Haaa thodi pagal hu lekin shayad koi pagal hi tumko itna pyaar

kar sakta hai

Tum mere waqt se guzar gaye lekin main apne daur main hu
Firse sunlo
Main mohabbat bewajah karungi tumse bepanah karungi
tumse betahashaa karungi tumse behadd karungi tumse.
- Prachi Ajay Dhoke

Prachi Ajay Dhoke

Hii!, I'm Prachi Ajay Dhoke I'm a Student, Choreographer, Stand up Comedian, Memer, and an executive assistant of managing director in a branding company, I'm 4'9 because I am carrying huge responsibilities on my little shoulder. I'm limitless so i don't care about boundaries. I'm here for smiles, in the decade of sorrows, I'll make you feel like home.

98. Gehraiyaan

Rote hue asu aks se bahe jainge tu wapas na bulana maa
Firse wahi sare khwab tere adhure rai jainge maaa!
Mai akhri tak tere akho ka tara raha tha maa mujhe pata hai ,
Lekin sirf tere asu mujhe kaha leker wapas aainge.
Bhagwan ke pas gaya hu mai unse ek baat jarur puchunga maa,
Bhagwan tu hai yaa meri maa ?
Jawab dete hui bhagwan bhi pachtainge naa ,
Aj maa ke asu unhe bhi rulainge naa!
Maa tere asu se meri ruhhh kap jati hai
Andar se wapas tere pas ane ki awaj ati hai !
Maa tu kitni bholi hai tujhe pata hai mai wapas nahi aunga
naa,
Lekin tere man me chalrahaa ke sham hotee hi tera beta ghar
aainga naa,
Tu bholi hai maa tere aage sansar bhi jukh jaingaa ,
tera beta wapas nahi aainga !
Lekin khuda is baat per jarur pachtainga.
Lekin khuda is baat per jarur pachtainga!
- Aman Sheikh

Aman Sheikh

|| art movement ||

99. Untitled Love

We were drunk in love, we were clenching wine's goblet in our hands, feet were palpitating, there was nebulous on our face but there was equally a feel of ecstasy. That day two moons were spreading the effulgence.

On attaining the pinnacle of the mountain, the sorrows of life fluctuates to a short form, because at that time we are abstracted from humanistic life

The amplitude of mountains is much ginormous. sorrow is as if a crumpled stone in front of them and we don't know how many such sorrows a mountain suffers!

Nature is hushed, performs a special dance in solitude, a elated dance!

But don't you worry, we will be impuissant to see it forever, because our happiness is only to enjoy the opulences.

It is inherent to be carnal in love. The carnality takes birth just after the first meeting, because it is not possible to spontaneously fall in intimate relationship with a stranger found on the road, but the union of the body is not shallow, it is an undertaking that destroys the pleasure of lust . God creates man, gives form, gives breath, gives a dying body

But love?

It is born out of primordial longing, for the believers it is a divine boon and for the atheists, it is the sound of the body. Aeons will pass but physicality and love will not be able to separate, comrade!

- Ravi Avasthi

Ravi Avasthi

Having few steps with words.

100. An Hour Of Realisation.

Kuch to baat hain
iss waqt mein,
Jo mujhe aasman
mein dekhne ko
Majboor karti hai ,
Jaise mujhse keh rahi ho
"Ki tu dekh daal sapne,
Himmat hai wo tujhme"

Wo dheeme dheeme chidiyo ki chachahahat ,
Dheere dheere jaise mere kaano may guftagoo kar rahi ho ,
""Ho gayi bahut der,
Ab uth ja thodi der,
Utha apne pankh aur
Bhar le apne sapno ki
udaan!""
Wo roshni bhara andhera mujhme ek vishwas ka
deepak jala raha hai ki,
Fir ek subha hone ko hai,
Fir ek mauka Milne ko hai,

Fir ek kadam badhane ko hai,
Fir kuch nayi sikh milne ko hai,
Ho ja tayar tu kyuki ,
Fir ek subah hone ko hai.
- Aayushi Manchanda

Aayushi Manchanda

Hey, This is Aayushi (with double A) named as a_silentonserver on instagram, who just love observing every minute things, and like quoting them, without giving a second thought as her mind satisfaction matters more than anyone's approval. She is living the journey of her life, without wondering about the destination, as you know "Manzilo se jyda maza to safar ka hain", to bas wahi safar main hain wo.